Pick A Struggle

Cupcake

Seasons

Written By
Alana Marie

Alana Marie

In Gratitude

With every creative story, comes a muse, whose inspiration is so essential to the creation of the tale, that without them, the narrative would not exist. For me, that muse is the consolidation of countless characters from my life, including family, friends and loved ones, both here on earth along with those who have passed.

My dear mother, Helen, left this earth in May of 2012, never realizing that the morals, principles and standards which she had instilled in me, would result in a series of books, containing stories that would inspire so many others. She would be proud to hold in her strong yet gentle hands a brand new copy of this book, filled with my words and her lessons. I am sure she would read the pages of my stories time and again, bending down the corners to mark her favorite passages. Helen would undoubtedly carry the book in her very large purse, pulling it out whenever possible to brag to her friends about her daughter "the author". Mom, I thank you for everything you ever did for me. I love you today, tomorrow and always.

Let's fast forward to 2014, as fate steps in and orchestrates my unexpected introduction to Shari Yantes; the woman who would forever change my life. It may be corny to contend, as others have, that destiny brought us together to "save the world" but we both know in our hearts that we needed to find one another, just to save ourselves. Shari, a remarkable friend, mentor and companion encourages me daily to put pen to paper and release the words which fill up my soul. Together, we have fashioned an intense bond that is so deep and profound that we are astounded at times as we speak, think and dream the same things. Snowflake, I adore you and I am so grateful to have been blessed with your love and generous compassion.

I must thank my sister Diana, who lives her life so very far away in miles, yet always, finds the time to support and encourage my dreams, despite how crazy they may appear to her very grounded and conventional realm of thinking.

I need to acknowledge Tiffany Fox for editing my narratives and molding my words into interesting paragraphs of correct and proper English. You have taught me so much in our short time together. Also, the delightfully, charming cover design was created by a fellow author and friend, Judy Liautaud. Thank you ladies, for a job well done!

Finally, I must never forget to recognize you, my loyal readers, who hungrily devour all that I compose and wait excitedly for more. Your praises are humbling and they motivate me to write late into the dark of night. Without all of you, there would be no purpose for my stories and no reason to write even a single word. So thank you all from the bottom of my being. You have given me a wonderful opportunity to do something that I truly love and I hope that I, in turn, have given you a smile or two.

Enjoy the stories contained within these pages, for they were written just for you.

CONTENTS

A Reason For the Season

Have you realized yet, that each and every day you write a page from the story of your life? Your mind's eye captures all it sees, while your heart preserves all it feels, and these treasured memories are stowed away for future reference. The four seasons mark the chapters and divide the experiences, making it easier to recall the occasions and occurrences of our existence. Are your pages filled with the orange sherbet sunsets and cotton candy clouds of summer? Can you recall the vibrant colors of the maple trees in autumn? You know, the crimson red and golden leaves which drift past the pumpkins sleeping in the field as they await the fall harvest? Do they chronicle the delicate snowflakes and dripping icicles of winter or the warm family traditions of Christmas, Hanukkah, and New Year's Eve? Have you ever stared into the late night sky and watched the twinkling stars blink on and off to the rhythm of the north wind rushing past? With the passing of the winter solstice, we find blissful joy in starting fresh and the delightful opportunity to grow our hopes and aspirations. We smile proudly as we watch our dreams bud and bloom amidst the wildflowers and sapling trees of spring. Pay attention to the seasons for they are filled with enchanting magic and have priceless lessons to instill.

Pick a Struggle Cupcake- Seasons is the second installment of *The Pick a Struggle Cupcake* series of short stories and life lessons created by its author Alana Marie. The tales and yarns are based on actual events which have occurred in her very colorful life. Once a five-hundred pound nightclub owner possessing a serious infatuation with alcohol who just happens to be a lesbian, Alana has had to overcome tremendous obstacles throughout the years. In sharing her experiences in a raw yet sensitive fashion, she hopes to inspire, provoke, and motivate others to take the steps necessary to chase their dreams and overcome their own struggles. Now my friend, go find a quiet corner, open this book, and indulge yourself with a delectable treat.

Alana Marie

Appreciate the Little Things

"Take a look back at your life and learn to forgive the people you love for the mistakes they have made. Don't forget to include yourself, as you see you have made quite a few, as well."

With spring we find another year and a new beginning. Appreciate the little things, marvel at the big. It is never too late to start again and again, and yet again. The secret to reaching your goal, losing weight, or finding success is persistence. Realize that your heart grows along with age, making room for tolerance, mercy, and compassion. Take a look back at your life and learn to forgive the people you love for the mistakes they have made. Don't forget to include yourself, as you see *you* have made quite a few, as well. Loyalty is more than just a word... it is an instinct you are born with. You can't be a *little* loyal any more than you can be a *little* sorry—either you are or you aren't. Honor your real friends. You will find you might have over two thousand Facebook friends; however, your *real* friends can be counted on one hand, two if you're lucky. As time slips past, there will be lovers and lost loves. At times, you will think about the ones you *thought* you loved and shed a tear over the one you *know* you loved... and then lost. Often times, you will sit and ponder over what lies ahead while believing the best has passed. Today is a day of reflection. Tomorrow will be a time of change. There will be turning points as you embrace the excitement of a new journey on the horizon. Ignore the anxious feeling inside, even if it makes your heart pound and your mind race. Dare to dream. Take the chance to explore the unknown and see the unseen. No one ever knows what's up ahead, but you have already lived the life behind you. There's no turning back. The joy and the wonders of life are always just out of reach. Never stop searching, learning, or loving. Learn to appreciate every single moment of your life for you will never, *ever* have enough.

The Easter Basket

"She dreamed of chocolate, licorice, and red jelly beans so when she opened her eyes at four in the morning, Easter candy was still on her mind."

Shelia bounced her rusted Chevy into the Walmart parking lot, circling the front of the store several times in search of a parking spot close to the front doors. Spotting an elderly woman getting into her car, Shelia rolled up behind her, waiting to pounce on the front row spot as soon as the blue-haired senior managed to back her massive Buick out. Once settled into the spot, she took a deep breath, opened the car door, and heaved herself out into the unprotected and hostile world of daylight. Shelia immediately felt the staring, watchful eyes settle upon her as she stood, quavering and holding on to the side of her car for support. When her legs finally gathered the strength to transport her massive four hundred fifty pound frame across the lot, she searched with determination for an empty shopping cart to serve as a makeshift walker to get her into the building. Spotting one, she hobbled over to the basket, breathing a sigh of relief as her hands finally gripped the cold, plastic-covered handle and she felt steady enough to make it to the front doors.

Shelia had decided to venture out today because her sister, Sarah, insisted on bringing her daughter over for a visit on Easter

Sunday. Sweet little Molly was her only niece. With soft golden curls and aqua blue eyes, she was such a lovely little girl. Shelia had once imagined having a child of her own… maybe even two. Jacob and Julia she would have named them. That desire had long since faded, though, with her food addiction stealing yet another of her dreams. It was ridiculous to even consider having a baby at her current weight as it would probably kill her. Besides, she seriously doubted she could find someone who could see past her enormous size and love her enough to want to have a child with her. Shaking the thoughts from her mind, she concentrated on the task at hand, building an incredible Easter basket for darling Molly.

Lumbering her way through the aisles, she made her way to the holiday section which was filled with beautiful straw baskets, plush, pink and yellow bunnies, and candy… oh, so much delectable, delightful, decadent candy! Suddenly, she felt a bit light-headed as she rounded the corner and found herself surrounded by shelves of Easter candy. Shelia first grabbed a large pink and white basket from the display, along with a bag of green plastic grass, and tossed them into the cart, eager to begin the candy selection. With her eyes scanning the shelves, she reached for all of her own personal favorites, confident that Molly would enjoy them, as well. The shopping cart began to fill with a mountain of treats including, Peeps, Cadbury Eggs, Jelly Beans, chocolate covered marshmallow bunnies, Robin Eggs, Malted Milk Balls, and last but not least, her favorite… Hershey Kisses covered, of course, in shiny pastel foils. Satisfied with her abundant selection, she wheeled the cart toward the registers when she realized she had forgotten the most important thing! Trudging back to the candy aisle, she looked for the giant chocolate rabbits. Reaching for a beautiful bunny she knew Molly would love, covered in shiny foil in a bright yellow box, she was disappointed to find it was hollow and weighed next to nothing. In all actuality, it would have been perfect since there was so much other candy for the basket, but Shelia dropped the box back onto the shelf and walked further until she found a one pound, solid chocolate rabbit that wasn't quite as pretty but three times as filling!

As Shelia stood in line, her legs began to ache while her feet throbbed inside of her shoes and she wondered if she had the strength to hold on until her turn to be cashed out. Ignoring the judgmental stares and the snickering children, she began to place her mounds of candy on the conveyer. Seventy-eight dollars later, she was on the move again, rolling toward the car. Overwhelmed and out of breath, she opened the back door and chucked the bags of candy on the backseat, managing to snag the bag of chocolate kisses before slamming the door shut. Shelia tossed the bag on the passenger seat and proceeded to shove and push herself in behind the steering wheel. Before she had even turned the key in the ignition, her shaking hand reached over and grabbed the bag of candy, tearing it open in one swift motion and with lightning-fast speed, she began unwrapping the first kiss. Closing her eyes, she popped the chocolate into her mouth and smiled as the candy coated her taste buds. A sense of calm tranquility filled her soul for but a moment and then she began frantically tearing the wrappers off handfuls of the candy. Half of the bag was already gone as she pulled out of the parking place, setting off for home. The bag was completely empty by the time she got there.

Feeling a little nauseous, Shelia wobbled into the house, carrying the rest of the Easter bounty. The massive dose of sugar entering her system made her feel dizzy, much like a few quick shots of whiskey had done back in her college days. A quick nap was in order and then Shelia would create an unforgettable Easter basket Molly would never forget!

Waking up four hours later, surrounded by darkness, Shelia decided it was too late to make dinner so she ordered and extra-large, double cheese pizza from Antonio's and set to the task of putting together the basket. Carefully, she placed each bag of luscious candy on the coffee table in front of her and oddly enough, felt a bit giddy. After spreading the grass around the bottom of the basket, she carefully arranged the candy inside. She picked up a leftover Peep and placed the soft yellow marshmallow in her mouth, where it melted on her tongue. The taste created a craving for more sugar and she began mechanically shoving piece after delectable piece of Molly's candy into her mouth.

When the pizza finally arrived, Shelia was so full that she

could only force down four pieces. Feeling full enough to burst, she settled back into her easy chair and drifted off to sleep once again. She dreamed of chocolate, licorice, and red jelly beans so when she opened her eyes at four in the morning, Easter candy was still on her mind. The basket sat proudly on the table in front of her. She stared at it intently and then tried not to look at it, for the cravings had begun. Eventually, her eyes were drawn back to the pretty pink basket and she gave into the urge to grab just a handful of malted milk balls, followed by a marshmallow rabbit or two, when suddenly, her willpower came crashing down upon her as she grabbed bits and pieces from the basket and then handfuls, cramming it all into her mouth before common sense forced her to stop! Finally, the basket was empty and feeling thoroughly disgusted with herself, she got up and waddled off to bed to collapse into a peaceful sugar coma.

The next afternoon, Shelia awoke with a headache, feeling repulsed and sickened by her actions of the night before as she sat in her chair staring at Molly's empty Easter basket. She looked on the floor and saw the Walmart bag sitting there with the giant one pound chocolate rabbit hiding inside. *Well now*, she thought to herself, *at least we still have something left for Molly*. She pulled the last shred of Easter candy out of the bag and set it on the table in front of her. It stood there, staring at her as she tried to watch the TV. The temptation to eat the rabbit began to overwhelm her. Her efforts to ignore the chocolate creature were fruitless and then suddenly, without warning, she snatched the box off the table and ripped it open, biting off his ears with a vengeance. She sat there and consumed the entire one pound rabbit in a single sitting as a feeling of serenity enveloped her. After a moment or two of uncomfortable silence, she looked at her watch and decided there was just enough time for a quick nap before she ventured back to Walmart to buy another batch of candy to refill that darn Easter basket... again.

Jackal

"The girls screamed as he moved across the stage, plucking dollar bills from their outstretched hands or their pouting lips, and he loved it. He loved every stinking second of it."

Jack looked into the mirror and studied his square jaw and good-looking features. He was quite pleased with the five o'clock shadow which had finally filled in on the sides of his face. Outside of the small cinderblock dressing room, he could hear the pounding beat of the evening overture which signaled the start of the show. Adrenaline rushed through his body as he stepped out on stage, where he stood, discreetly hidden behind the heavy, red velvet curtain. The emcee could be heard enticing the crowd to call his name. "Jackal…Jackal…Jackal…" And as the voices grew louder and more intense, he felt his heart begin to pound in his chest until suddenly, the curtains flew open and a thunderous roar filled the club. Jack stood there, alone on stage, with his back to the darkened audience, waiting impatiently for the first note of his signature song to burst through the massive sound system. There wasn't an empty seat in the house, in fact, standing room only; he could tell without even looking.

The Legacy had been his home bar for seven years. It was the club that had given him his first opportunity at 'drag.' Jack, aka Jackie, had been an awkward, eighteen-year-old tomboy showing off on the dancefloor, when one of the seasoned kings had noticed her. Tommy D. offered to take her under his wing and teach her the art of male illusion. Jack accepted the offer and had quickly gone on to become a headliner at The Legacy and a top paid performer in clubs all over the tristate area. Now, here he was, stepping out onto the stage for the final time. It all seemed strange and surreal and it felt like his world was about to come crashing down upon him.

All at once, the pounding drums of Def Leppard filled the room and he began jumping in place to the guitar riff at the beginning of

Pour Some Sugar on Me. The crowd leapt to its feet as Jackal spun around and the white-hot spotlight engulfed him. He felt comfort in the heat on his face and his blinded vision. The girls screamed as he moved across the stage, plucking dollar bills from their outstretched hands or their pouting lips, and he loved it. He loved every stinking second of it. For so many years, the stage was the only place he felt at home; it made him feel like the man he should have always been.

Jack lived for the weekend, wishing he could just sleep through the other five days. Instead, he flipped burgers in Uncle Milton's diner every day from ten a.m. until close. The front door of the place opened to a shiny, stainless steel counter surrounded by a

row of cherry red vinyl stools. Large, comfy, red booths outlined the room with gleaming white Formica tables inside. As you stepped through the front door, you were greeted by the sound of sizzling burgers and the roar of French fries dropping into vats of bubbling oil. The smell of food was intoxicating and the mysterious recipe of Uncle Milton's secret "Gut-Buster" kept the place hopping. Jack had grown up in that diner and could fondly remember Aunt Nellie dropping quarters in the old Wurlitzer jukebox and encouraging him—as an enthusiastic seven-year-old—to dance and sing for the customers. Jack, who knew the words to every single worn out forty-five, did so happily, since he was eager to please his favorite aunt, especially when the delighted customers tossed him dimes and quarters at the end of each song. That was his first taste of stardom and at the time, he had no idea how performing would one day change his entire life.

Back on stage, the infamous Jackal continued to relish in what would be his last time in the spotlight. The audience, knowing this was indeed his final curtain call, kept the applause going throughout the entire performance, hoping maybe it would help change his mind and postpone the inevitable. It would not. Jack knew the time had come to put his drag career behind him, especially since it wasn't really 'drag' anymore. A little over a year ago, Jack had made the decision to transition. Tired of living a lie, Jack worked hard and saved his money—*all* of his money. After investigating clinics and doctors, procedures and techniques, he had decided to move forward with the process of Testosterone injections even though some of the possible side effects could be quite severe. The transformation began quickly as his voice began to change and his soft facial features hardened. He felt dizzy with excitement the morning he woke to discover budding facial hair on his cheek and chin. Jack spent late nights working out in his basement, developing a new body and physique. There had been bouts with nausea, allergic reactions, mood swings, and hot flashes but he would not change a thing, never once questioning his choice to move forward with his transformation.

As Jackie became Jack, there seemed to be no place in his life for the persona of Jackal. With his top surgery complete and his bottom surgery scheduled, combined with the official name and gender change yesterday afternoon at the DMV, he was not a 'male impersonator' anymore. He was a man. The stage had once provided an outlet for his alter ego to shine and a safe and welcoming place to be himself. It was a teeny, tiny spot in a callous, intolerant world where he was applauded for his courage and conviction. He now had the whole world to conquer, discover, and explore. There was no longer a need to tape down or 'pack up.' The facial hair was real, and the heart and soul had *finally* found harmony within the vessel in which they traveled. It was time to let go of the safety net Jackal had provided.

The song ended to a massive wave of love and applause as the crowd screamed "Encore! Encore!" Jackal stood there fascinated, enchanted by this single, powerful moment that would end an era. Soaking up the spotlight and surveying the room one last time, Jack considered an encore but decided against it. After all, Aunt Nelly had always said "Leave 'em wanting more!" And that's just what he did as he bowed one last time and walked off the stage.

An Adventurous Soul

"I felt like a baby bird who so craved flight, only to find they were indeed a bird but a penguin whose feet would never leave the earth."

I have an adventurous soul. The fact it has remained inert, tucked away inside of a massive, dormant body for twenty-five years, doesn't change the reality that it *does* exist. When I was but a child, I would watch the planes fly overhead and wonder where they were headed as they soared across the magnificent blue sky. I, myself, dreamed of boarding one of those airplanes with no destination in mind, just the possibility of finding rippling ocean waves plunging across a white, sandy shore at the end of the voyage. Perhaps it would transport me over majestic, snow-capped mountains to distant countries, unfamiliar places full of exotic individuals who might introduce me to peculiar foods and colorful customs. The possible destinations seemed infinite and eternal, yet I seldom traveled beyond my backyard. World travelers had to be strong, healthy, and adventurous. At five hundred pounds, I was none of these. Exploring new lands involved climbing, hiking, and walking, but first, it usually involved flying. For me, this created a problem. Five-hundred-pound tourists do not ride in airplanes simply because they cannot squeeze their bulky bodies into the tiny seats. So I discovered, to my great disappointment, all of the great adventures I had imagined would have to wait. The excessive weight I carried served as an anchor, holding me down and close to the ground for more than two decades. I felt like a baby bird who so craved flight, only to find they were indeed a bird but a penguin whose feet would never leave the earth.

There came a day when I felt a longing in my soul so great, I began to hunger for something other than the food which had come to control me. It was a yearning so intense, it spoke to my heart. It asked for the freedom to fly, which in turn, gave me hope. I dared to dream of what it might be like to one day feel the wind beneath my wings and the breeze in my hair. Something profound happened that fateful day. I took the first step of what would be a long, lonesome journey of struggle and sadness. The voyage consumed my life. I pushed forward, one painful step after another. After a time, I developed a steady stride and moved forward at a brisker pace which made my days a bit brighter. As the worst days of my life began to pile up behind me, I started to feel the progress of my determination and then one unexpected day, it happened! My courage surpassed my apprehension and I bought a ticket. The destination was not exceedingly important but the triumph of completing the journey would be invaluable.

The night before my maiden flight, my heart fluttered and my mind raced as I filled my brand new suitcase with all of the things I had imagined other practiced travelers might pack. I lay in bed that night, staring at the ceiling. When my alarm clock went off at seven a.m., my eyes were still open but I felt more energized and alive than I could ever remember feeling. The anxiety held on and my heart continued to beat wildly as my darkest memories of the past came back to plague me. My biggest fear was not being small enough to fit into the modest airplane seats. I may have reduced myself to a two-hundred-eighty-pound body but I still carried around that five-hundred-pound self-image. As I boarded the plane and made my way to my appointed seat, I felt beads of sweat on the back of my neck and feared my knees might give out during the walk down the aisle. I stood there looking at the seat for what seemed like an eternity, when suddenly, another passenger cleared his throat behind me. Startled, I took a deep breath, closed my eyes, and aimed my generous-sized rear end between the arm rests. I slid down into the seat quite snugly, but I FIT! My dear God… I really fit! I pulled the seatbelt around my waist and snapped it securely into place. The fear and apprehension drained from my body like air from a balloon and I relaxed and shut my eyes as the engines fired up and the massive plane began to coast down the runway. Once we had ascended and the plane had leveled itself, I bravely stole a glance out the window next to me. I suddenly comprehended with utter amazement that I had to look *down* to see the clouds. At that very moment, it occurred to me just how much courage and strength it had taken to rise above my world of doubt, shame, and reservation and find myself there, *literally* above the clouds. I truly understood, for the first time in my life, the meaning of "The sky is the limit!" To me, with my newfound wings, it signifies opportunity is boundless, possibilities are endless, and the sky has no constraints. Floating there, above the earth, I felt weightless, hopeful, and free as I realized *anyone* can fly once they discover the courage to try.

Returning to Learning

"The morning I mounted my doctor's freight scale to discover I had become a member of the one percent of the world population to exceed the five-hundred pound mark had felt like the worst day of my life; little did I know that it was only the beginning of a horrendous nightmare."

I sit on this cold, hard bench, holding the unopened envelope in my hand, thinking about the year I have been through. Confusion, stress, and chaos come to mind. I recall a few good times but many more days best forgotten. There is a sense of accomplishment as far as having the nerve to return to a university after thirty years away, yet there is that uneasy feeling which encompasses me—one of being lost, alone, and isolated. The inquisitive, chubby brown squirrel who stares sideways at me is surely thinking about how out of place I look. "What are you doing here?" he wonders. I wonder that myself. I really don't belong. This campus is filled with youthful broods of adolescent prodigies and computer wizards. They swarm and buzz around me while I stare at my phone, struggling to open a Yahoo message from my fifteen-year-old niece. The seasons, the semesters, even the students are in transition. I am in transition, as well. They pass from spring into summer, while I single-handedly face what is most certainly a brutal winter ahead. I am pleased with the perfect 4.0 grade point average I have maintained for two semesters but I am also saddened by the realization I cannot afford to return for classes in the fall.

The stillness of the campus on this fine spring day is delightful. Such a beautiful place when all of the brassy youngsters are in their classrooms learning about the things I, myself, have already lived through. Again, I wonder why I am here. Do I have something to prove, and to whom? I'd spent years locked away with my soul buried inside of a two-hundred-fifty-pound security blanket which nearly stole my life as it tiptoed in and systematically embezzled my days, weeks, and years. A decade had disappeared before I was forced to wake up and take notice. The morning I mounted my doctor's freight scale to discover I had become a member of the one percent of the world population to exceed the five-hundred pound mark had felt like the worst day of my life; little did I know that it was only the beginning of a horrendous nightmare. The nurse nervously avoided eye contact and my heart sank as she wrote the staggering number on her clipboard. It felt like a prison sentence had been handed to me... a life sentence, in fact. Much of the next year I'd spent hidden away in my apartment, feeling helpless and alone while relentlessly and tenaciously eating myself to death.

Losing the weight had honestly been a fierce battle for my life. Counseling, Weight Watchers, and a frightful fear of my own mortality had carried me through the three-year battle to lose the massive poundage I'd carried so doggedly on my back. The little miracles and milestones I'd conquered along the journey— walking, camping, and fitting into a movie theatre seat—led me to crave more functional freedom, which in turn brought me joy again for the first time in years. I had forgotten how to smile just as I had forgotten how to live. Getting back in school had been the carrot at the end of a very long stick. It became my goal, my prize, my future, and even more importantly, my freedom. When the funds ran out, so did my optimism and motivation. On a whim one day, I applied for a scholarship in the Creative Writing Department. The youngster at the financial aid desk who'd handed me the stack of paperwork smiled and said, "Well, don't put all your eggs in this basket. After all, only one percent of the kids... err... I mean, people who apply actually get accepted." Stopping in my tracks, I turned around and looked at her, stating curtly, "One percent, huh? Well, little one, it won't be my first struggle with that statistic." With that, I turned and walked out into the hallway, hiding my dismay at her dismal prognosis.

Weeks had passed since I'd turned in my scholarship application and in all honesty, I'd given up on even hearing back from them. One percent is, in fact, a very daunting number. But here today, I hold in my hand a very thin envelope from the University Financial Aid Office. Breathing in the crisp morning air, I realize subconsciously that I am saying goodbye. I rationalize with myself that this was but a single dream plucked from oh so many others still waiting to be accomplished. The eternal list I'd compiled could, in fact, keep me diligently occupied for a lifetime, so why fret over this one setback? As I began to tear open the envelope, I still wondered why? Suddenly, the truth hit me. I was a success, a winner, a remarkable student. I had always known there was so much to learn, but in going back to school I'd come to realize I had even more to teach! Perhaps I had found my calling... my justification for suffering, for hurting all of these miserable years, but more importantly, my reason for being. My heart pounded as I slipped the letter out of the envelope.

Congratulations it read and without even reading another word, I knew. I clutched the letter to my chest, realizing in that single significant moment, I was releasing my past and embracing my future. I had arrived but even more than that... I had survived.

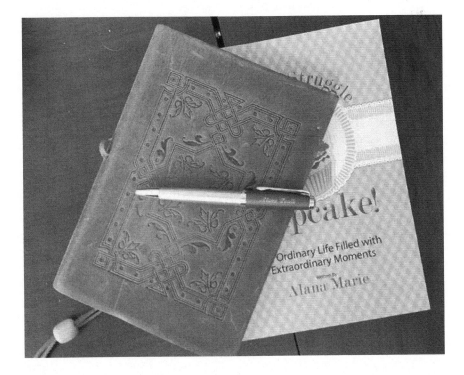

When Everything Changed

"She sat down on the floor, cross-legged, in the middle of the empty waiting area. She thought at first that she might begin to cry, but the tears did not come."

Autumn stood, waiting impatiently outside the glass doors of the Delta arrival gate. Her hand shook just a bit as she slid the last Marlboro Light out of the pack. As she fumbled through her sweatshirt pocket, searching hastily for a lighter, she was reminded of the promise she had made to herself to quit smoking. She had, in fact, stopped for almost six months but the events of the day had triggered a relapse. *Well, this is really* it—*the final smoke, the last cigarette of my life,* she vowed as she lit the tip of her Marlboro and inhaled deeply. Autumn strode along the sidewalk until she reached an aluminum bench next to the red brick building. Tired of standing, she plopped down onto the chilly seat and her mind drifted back to an icy cold January evening and a conversation which had occurred in her little, one-bedroom Colorado apartment.

"Tell me you aren't really thinking of keeping it!" he had shouted at her, the confrontation sounding more like a threat than a question. Those appalling words had sent a chill through her veins and bounced around inside of her head for weeks after he'd unleashed them. Staring into his cold, hard eyes, she could not find a single trace of the man she'd fallen in love with nearly two years ago.

Upon meeting, there had been an intense physical attraction between them. Randy, drawn first to her unpretentious, subtle beauty, later found her brazen tongue and cheeky attitude alluring in a curious, inexplicable way. Autumn, on the other hand, had so enjoyed the cat and mouse game she skillfully played with this dark and handsome stranger, even though it had been love at first sight on her part. Playing 'hard to get' became exceedingly difficult as their effortless physical attraction for one another turned to passionate desire. They became intimate, inseparable, and undividable. Friends and family frowned upon their youthfulness and the intensity of their romance, telling them to slow down. Tired of the scrutiny and looking for adventure, there came a day when they hatched a plan to move out west. Colorado seemed a pleasant destination. Minnesota had become boring, monotonous, and dreary. Craving excitement and freedom, the pair rented a U-Haul that spring, packed it up, and gleefully said goodbye to everything and everyone they had ever known.

Initially, the excitement of the adventure was intoxicating. On this journey, they had discovered a newfound freedom they had never been afforded and with that liberty came the ability to make their own choices, some of which happened to be very poor decisions. They found an apartment on the seedy side of town where they discovered a new collection of cronies and cohorts who enjoyed a good time more than a quiet life. The group of very young adults partied hard and heavy which made keeping a job a difficult task. Autumn had found and lost four jobs in just as many months. Randy worked on and off for a bit, in fact, just enough to keep the lights on and the landlord off his back. Eventually, the good times turned to difficult times. Their lack of money fueled a fire of discontent, and their laid-back, easygoing relationship began to crumble.

Autumn savored the last drag of her final cigarette and sighed as she blew out the smoke and dropped the butt onto the sidewalk beneath her feet. She flattened the glowing embers as she stood up to head inside. Looking at her watch, it was seven p.m. The plane was due to arrive shortly and her nerves would no longer tolerate the stillness of sitting motionless on the bench. She strolled into the terminal to warm up and once again, wait. As she walked aimlessly through the building, her thoughts began to wander again as she recalled her visit to the cold, sterile room she'd been seated in at the Denver free clinic. "Congratulations," the doctor had said with an apprehensive smile, "you're going to have a boy… a strong, healthy boy." Autumn's heart had stopped and she had felt as though she might faint right there in the office. She had felt so conflicted at the time. Her heart raced with unmitigated, eager excitement while her mind flooded itself with nervous apprehension. She'd done it this time. There would be no way to talk her way out of this mess.

As the weight began to settle on her once petite frame, and the morning sickness replaced the pre-baby hangovers, Autumn knew she could no longer hide this ruinous secret from Randy. This predicament would not just go away. She began to wonder if the news of this baby—*his* baby—might bring them closer. Perhaps he would be overjoyed or at least happy at the thought of having a son? She had decided to share the news that night and predictably, Randy was far from overjoyed. He sat there on the sofa, breathing heavy, arms crossed, staring at her as if she were Satan. He huffed and sighed and slammed his head onto the back of the couch, squeezing his eyes closed. There were no hugs or smiles and the room began to feel suffocating with gloom and despair. Autumn could say, with definite certainty, she had indeed reached the lowest point of her life at that very moment. Her world came crashing down as Randy's next comment spewed from his mouth. "What are you thinking? My God, we can barely feed ourselves!" he shouted as he stood up and stormed out of the tiny apartment, slamming the door behind him. For a moment, she wondered if maybe Randy was right. She had no idea how to raise a baby. Perhaps she should get rid of the baby, or at least give it to someone who could afford to take care of it. Autumn felt the tears well up and finally burst from her eyes. She sat there, alone in the apartment, and continued to cry as the afternoon sun dropped from the sky. She fell asleep on the couch, waiting for Randy to return. She awoke to sunshine in her eyes and a silent, empty apartment. Autumn realized she needed her family and friends and it was time to go home. She reached for the phone and dialed her mother's number. They talked for hours, and that afternoon, she found herself soaring across the sky back to Minnesota.

The loudspeaker lit up the room with the announcement that Delta flight 377 from Denver had landed, abruptly jerking Autumn back to the present moment. Her heart beat wildly as her eyes searched the terminal for his face, even though, in all reality, he could not have even gotten off the plane yet. She began to speculate if maybe she should have brought the baby in with her for this little family reunion. She had considered it, but had decided the airport was not where she wanted father and son to meet. David, or little DJ for short, was outside waiting in the car with his grandmother. She had only contemplated bringing him in because Randy had missed so much already. Autumn had elected to remain in Minnesota with her family and have the baby there. Finding herself away from judgmental eyes and negative accusations, it became clear to her that although she was petrified beyond belief, she could never, *ever* give up this baby. They had stayed in contact through the pregnancy, attempting graciously to work their issues out, but things were different now. Something had changed. Well, no, *everything* had changed, including Autumn.

The passengers began filing through the gate as she waited with anxious anticipation. They flowed into the terminal in a steady wave of people, but Randy was nowhere to be seen. Autumn's head began to swim as the wave turned into a trickle and eventually, no one else came through the gate. And still she waited, hoping he would come running to her, smiling that unforgettable smile she had fallen in love with, and cover her face with kisses… dozens of loving kisses. She stood there in sad disbelief and her knees grew weak. She sat down on the floor, cross-legged, in the middle of the empty waiting area. She thought at first that she might begin to cry, but the tears did not come. Instead, she felt strength inside like she had never felt before. Feeling silly sitting there, she pulled herself to her feet and marched out the door to her mother's waiting car.

As she approached the vehicle and saw her mother's concerned face, she wished in vain she had saved one last cigarette. But that craving disappeared as soon as she saw her little DJ strapped in his car seat. Autumn opened the back door and lifted him out of the seat, feeling an overwhelming sensation of emotion fill her heart. She hugged him to her chest and smelled the delicate, musky smell of his hair and now, the tears did fall. She was suddenly overwhelmed by the infinite amount of love she felt for this tiny human being. This innocent child, who looked up at her with eyes identical to her own and a hint of his daddy's irresistible smile, and she knew *this* little man would love her forever. She realized, regrettably, that she had taken too many foolish risks in her life and made so many mistakes and bad choices, but this pure and beautiful child was not one of them. Randy would not be around to watch this incredible baby grow and thrive, but she would be there, always. No, she did not need Randy anymore, for she had fallen in love with another boy... a charming, handsome, eight-pound boy.

Shackles

"The yearning was perpetual, incessant and while it began, ever so silently to creep into my life, it wrapped me in a fatal grip much like the Black Widow spins a web around its weak and helpless prey. "

I felt it. That empty hollow chasm deep inside, the one which never seemed to fill. There it was, this hole in my soul. Its relentless cries of starvation absorbed my days and dominated my nights. The constant craving never left my thoughts, my notions, or even my dreams. The yearning was perpetual, incessant and while it began, ever so silently to creep into my life, it wrapped me in a fatal grip much like the Black Widow spins a web around its weak and helpless prey.

The uninvited predator boldly attacked my fragile mind like a bandit stealing first my hope, my dreams, and finally my freedom. And still, the longing remained; the incessant hunger for something, *anything*, to satiate that yearning within. Feeding the beast became my life purpose, a daily race with no tangible end. Endless hours of intense devouring and consuming in a feeble attempt to fill the abyss. It began to feel almost like an intravenous transfusion with the continual pumping of food into my system as if it were the only factor keeping me alive. In all reality, it was killing me. Slowly and relentlessly, it was stealing my life. The most ridiculous piece of this ghastly conundrum was the realization I was assisting the demon in my own forthcoming demise.

At last, when the incessant takeover paused for but a moment, I found the opportunity to consider my noxious, unhealthy predicament. I sat in isolated silence and contemplated, sadly, my own exodus. Then, quite abruptly, thoughts turned to a possible resurrection. My mind raced with unrelenting reasons for me to do combat with these horrendous demons. Something deep within had forbidden me to give up, to give in, or check out. Suddenly, I felt a desire I had not experienced in quite some time. It was a passion to live again—an overwhelming, intense yearning to regain my life. An excruciating hunger to feel the sun on my face and fresh air in my ravaged lungs forced me out of my chair and to the front door, which I flung open like a madwoman! The bright light nearly blinded me as I stumbled out into a magnificent world I had not visited in such a very long time. My heart pounded as I embraced the breathtaking energy which ignited my spirit. I stepped off of the porch and as I savored the cool, supple blades of summer grass between my toes, I felt the shackles relax as the blackness reluctantly surrendered its grip upon my soul

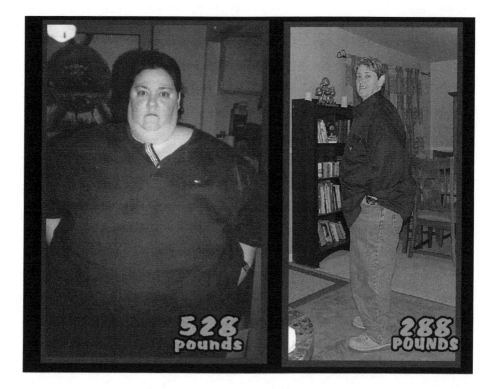

Fade To Black

"This would, indeed, be an instant in time shared by two, yet remembered by just one. With great sadness, I had considered the certain reality that this would be the last time I saw him... ever."

With his hand folded inside of mine, I sat beside him on the ancient queen-size bed we had shared for nearly eight years. As he lay sleeping, I rested silently and watched him breathe in a perfect, steady cadence, the soft and faded patchwork quilt rising and falling with each breath. So peaceful and content he appeared—probably caught up in a delightful dream—not realizing his life was about to change forever. The sad and probably most unforgiving piece of this whole scenario was the simple truth that he would never realize the finality of this single moment, until, of course, it was too late to amend it. This would, indeed, be an instant in time shared by two, yet remembered by just one. With great sadness, I had considered the certain reality that this would be the last time I saw him... ever.

He had been both my lover and my enabler and loved me so much he nearly killed me with all of his kindness. We had met when I weighed almost three hundred pounds and he had ridden beside me as the numbers on the scale climbed all the way up to four hundred fifty pounds. It seemed as though his love for me grew as I did. He carted in bags of fast food every time he came home from work and was always quick to make an ice cream or candy run. I suppose he only wanted to make me happy and realized the instant gratification food brought me did just that. He did not comprehend he was only feeding my addiction which left me feeling overwhelming sadness once the food was gone. The years slid past and the weight piled up. We both gained over a hundred pounds during the first two years.

Staring at his face, I acknowledged the fact that despite his enabling tendencies, he had not been a bad partner, for he had been dedicated, committed, and true blue and I was respectfully prepared to accept all blame for this break-up. Upon first consideration, my close and always loyal friends would blame the failed relationship on him while attempting to justify my leaving, but in all truth, it was me; I will concede and admit it. Surely, I could have stayed, for it wasn't a bad life; it just wasn't good enough. Others in our circle will criticize my decision, demanding to know the how and why of the split. Of course, he would demand answers from me, as well. I will not disclose, justify, or discuss the reason, for the truth would break his heart. I will, instead, steal away into the night, a coward, leaving all that was mine and ours as his. He will wake to find me gone… and he will cry.

There will, in every relationship, come a time when one or both individuals will find themselves at a crossroads. After so much time and energy has been exhausted trying to change the other person, you discover that you, yourself, have changed. Personally, I began to lose the weight I had accumulated through the years. I made getting fit and healthy my goal and successfully lost more than half of my body mass. As one's body changes, so do their mind, spirit, and attitude. You begin to weigh and measure moments, wondering if the time invested in your partner and your relationship is too valuable to lose. It is then you may realize the best of your days together lie behind you instead of before you. You will reflect and fantasize, daydream and visualize a tomorrow without each other. Eventually, you will find yourself fearless enough to collect the courage to stand up alone and walk away from all that has held you down and you will realize you would rather have something to look forward to than insignificant memories to look back on. It is at that moment you will begin to breathe again. You will stand up and take the first step into what will be an epic journey.

I knew it was my time, my adventure, and maybe my one and only chance at happiness. I stood up next to the bed and bent over and kissed his forehead as a single tear slipped down my cheek. I reach over and pulled the chain dangling from the little bedside lamp and at that moment, my life, my past, and any future we might have together faded to black. I walked out of the room, closed the door, and headed toward the light.

Reckless Abandon

"Am I really brave enough to leave my not-so-happy past behind? Am I fearless enough to abandon everything and everyone I have ever known to face the unknown with nothing but my wits and courage to guide me?"

Standing in the center of the room with her hands on her hips and an overwhelmed look on her face, she stared in silence at the plethora of boxes which flooded the living room floor. Beside her stood her faithful, little bronze-colored Chihuahua, Maggie, who sensed change was indeed in the making. Around them, brown cardboard cartons of every conceivable size sat yawning and open, waiting patiently for more precious cargo to be stacked and packed inside. The stream of keepsakes, knick-knacks, and superfluous souvenirs was never-ending and caused her to sigh in angst. Where had all of this stuff come from and more importantly, why on earth was she saving it? She realized, with anguish, that her home symbolized the excess she had yet to rid from her life.

Losing the weight had been most important. The extra two hundred fifty pounds she had carried around for so many years had nearly stolen her life and the extreme consumption of alcohol practically embezzled her soul. They had both played a part in her hopeless imprisonment and doing battle with each of them was like dueling with the devil. Three years of fighting with an iron will and a steel heart, she had triumphed, kicking the dickens out of both demons by getting sober and losing most of the excess weight. The only anchor weighing her down now was this huge old house overflowing with all of the stuff she had accumulated over the past several decades. It seemed as though the first half of her life had focused on gaining and obtaining more while today, her future begged her to remove, abandon, and discard the things restricting her independence.

Recently, she had made up her mind to begin a brand new journey with her streamlined body and this delightful new attitude on life. The lease on her home would expire soon and she had a destination or two in mind, so she had begun packing up the sprawling, four-bedroom ranch and found herself quite flabbergasted with the whole process. Most of the rooms had gone unused the entire time she had stayed there. There was a whole side of her home which reminded her of a dusty old museum filled with self-proclaimed treasures no one bothered to look at. Everything sat there, waiting in limbo for a purpose. Shelves of books remained unread alongside hundreds of movies encased in shiny, plastic boxes, seen once, and then crammed into the shelf, lost forever, never to be viewed again.

Woefully, she strolled into the sunny country kitchen. This room had actually been the one which had sold her on the house, and though she loved that kitchen, she had never learned to cook. Wearily, she glanced over at the massive box of pots in the corner filled with mismatched pans and lids and noticed the only one she ever used—an old red and black skillet with a worn out handle— still sat upon the stove, waiting to be packed. She grabbed it and perched it precariously on top of the leaning stack of steel and aluminum inside the box.

Feeling beleaguered, she moved quietly from room to room, taking note of the massive, heavy furniture crammed into every corner. She peeked into one of the extra bedrooms she had not visited in quite a while and shook her head at the expensive exercise equipment which was barely visible beneath the blanket of clothing that had been tossed upon it after several frantic, wardrobe search sessions.

In the closet, she spotted a large, worn, leather suitcase that had belonged to her mother. She pulled it from its hiding spot and carried it to her bedroom. She laid it upon the bed and began to fill the hollow shell with important things she did not want to get lost in the confusion of the move. A few photo albums stuffed with favorite pictures of family and friends went in first, followed by a pine jewelry box containing all of her favorite rings and things, including a few her mother had worn. There were trinkets and baubles inside, which she would never again wear, given to her by past lovers and admirers. Try as she might, she could not force herself to part with these silly mementos. She traced her finger around the edge of a silver pocket watch on a chain which had belonged to her father. The hands had stopped moving long ago, but just seeing the old timepiece warmed her heart. She opened the bottom drawer of her dresser and pulled out a stack of journals and a swollen, pink diary she had guarded with vigor since the seventh grade. She walked over to the nightstand and lifted a tarnished, silver photo frame which held her favorite photograph of her mother and herself taken on her mom's last Christmas upon this earth. She took a deep breath, hoping it might help to dry the tears welling up in her eyes as she silently replayed the holiday visit in her mind. Wrapping the frame in her favorite hooded sweatshirt and placing everything on top, she proceeded to close the suitcase full of treasures. As it snapped shut, she wondered to herself, *Am I really brave enough to leave my not-so-happy past behind? Am I fearless enough to abandon everything and everyone I have ever known to face the unknown with nothing but my wits and courage to guide me?*

Stepping out into the cool, quiet morning, she stood in silent serenity and stared at the magenta sky and the magnificent sunrise before her. At that particular moment, she made her decision. The weathered suitcase slipped easily into the backseat. Slamming the door, she turned and headed back up the walk toward the house which she had considered home for such a long time. Little Maggie felt the excitement in the air and turned madly in circles as her master stepped into the room. Bending down, she scooped up the eager Chihuahua, holding her tightly beneath one arm. She stood reflectively and glanced around the house one last time. Slowly, she began to back out of the front door when something caught her eye. She rushed past the open boxes which held all the suffocating baggage of her life and into the kitchen, where she reached out and grabbed the worn, comfortable handle of the red skillet and headed back out the front door, dropping the keys through the mail slot once she slammed it shut.

Setting Maggie down to ride shotgun in the passenger seat, she started her Mustang and smiled as Journey belted out "Don't stop believing" on the radio. The gravel crunched beneath the tires as she backed out of her drive for the final time. She fitted her sunglasses over her eyes, pointed her car toward the horizon, where the summer sun sat glowing like a bright orange balloon, pushed the accelerator to the floor, and left all she owned behind her in a cloud of dust.

The Voyage of the
Pistachio Green Bicycle

"As I pushed the kickstand down, a sense of guilt came over me, and I pondered the possibility of putting a "for sale" ad in the local paper. Perhaps, it was time to give up on this particular fantasy."

Dragging the last few bits and pieces of my previous life from the back of the nearly vacant moving van, a blanket slipped to the floor of the hollow box, revealing the long forgotten pistachio green bicycle. It stood there, dignified and proud, with its solid metal frame and huge white leather seat balanced securely on super-sized whitewall tires. The sturdy steed had survived the fourteen-hour trek across four states to its new home in Minnesota.

I stood and stared at the bike, realizing it had been almost a year since I had spotted her on the rack at the local Walmart and felt that "love at first sight" notion. It had been thirty-five years since I had ridden a bike, and truthfully, I believed my bike riding days were far behind me. Yet, after losing nearly two-hundred-fifty pounds over the past several years, I was feeling a bit optimistic that afternoon. I can still remember the hopeful enthusiasm I had felt in my heart that day as I rolled her past curious shoppers to the registers at the front of the store. When I arrived home that afternoon, I pulled the bike out of my car and set it down in my driveway, anxious to "take it for a spin." Still quite chubby, I found it extremely difficult to climb up in the seat and balance myself on what now seemed like two tiny tires. After a few attempts, I realized purchasing the bicycle was only half the battle; taking it for a ride would be the true victory.

On this particular day, while rolling it down the ramp of the moving van, I felt a tremendous sadness in my heart as I conceded to the reality, that after an entire year, I had still not mustered up enough courage to take the pistachio green bicycle for even a single jaunt. The initial dreams I had entertained of rolling down country roads with the wind in my face and the sun on my back had quickly turned to nightmares of fatal falls, broken bones, and certain humiliation. Today was no different. As I pushed the kickstand down, a sense of guilt came over me, and I pondered the possibility of putting a "for sale" ad in the local paper. Perhaps it was time to give up on this particular fantasy; after all, I had achieved so many other goals and aspirations since my massive weight loss, maybe riding a bike just wasn't meant to be. With a heavy heart, I rolled the bicycle to a dark corner of the cluttered garage and tossed a blanket upon her, subconsciously hoping out of sight really would put it out of my mind. I turned off the light and watched the heavy garage door close like a tomb, leaving the forsaken bicycle in complete darkness. I thought I had given up on my dream that day and then, quite unexpectedly and without warning, serendipity stepped in and the destiny of the pistachio green bicycle would forever change.

I met Coach Mona quite accidentally one afternoon during lunch with my partner, Shari. The muscular woman, who stood well over six feet tall, strode through the doors with magnificent confidence and seated herself at our table. Upon introductions, I was made aware of the fact she had been a college athlete superstar, an Olympic contender, and a professional basketball player. She had coached more than seventy-five teams and was currently a physical education instructor about to begin her twentieth year teaching. As could be expected, she was intrigued by my twenty-year battle with obesity. We had conversed for quite a while when the nearly forgotten pistachio green bicycle found its way into the conversation. It was only halfway through the tale when she hastily said, "Let's do this!" Startled by her abruptness, I stared at her in silence, not sure what turn the conversation had taken.

After a lengthy pep talk and motivational oration, Coach Mona had me quite convinced I could indeed ride the neglected bicycle and more than that, she would be there to teach, train, and coach me through it. Trust me when I tell you Coach Mona is not easily disregarded and does not accept no for an answer. Needless to say, Shari and I, along with Max, her eleven-year-old son, found ourselves standing in Mona's driveway that weekend, watching intently as she adjusted the pedals, seat, and handlebars for optimum comfort. Without much time for hesitation or uncertainty, she handed me a helmet and said, "Let's go!" My heart was pounding and my knees were shaking, but I knew I would never have a whole team behind me like this again, so I climbed, with great difficulty, into the driver's seat. Coach Mona held me up on one side and little Max did his best to hold up the other. Shari, never one to miss an opportunity for sharing an inspirational story, tenaciously manned the video camera, which turned out to be a marathon filming event!

Time after time, I relentlessly attempted to propel myself forward while turning the pedals beneath me. Desolate knees— which had not bent this far in decades—screamed in pain while sweat ran, unseen, down my back. As the sun rolled across the sky and the day slipped away, so did my hopes for even a fleeting ride on the dogged green bike. Everyone was sunburned and tired; however, no one but myself appeared ready to throw in the towel. Sensing my despair and anguish, Coach Mona pulled me aside for a pep talk and an ice cold bottle of water, and as could have been predicted, she coaxed me into one last attempt.

Rolling up my pant legs and tightening my helmet, I mounted the pistachio green bicycle for one last try. Placing my foot on the white, rubber pedal, I suddenly had a flashback to my childhood as my mother gripped the back of the seat of my first two-wheeler. I felt Coach Mona's hand dauntlessly replace hers on the back of my seat that hot July afternoon, but I sensed Mom's spirt lingering beside us as we took a deep breath and the wheels began to turn beneath me. In those few seconds, I found strength and courage like I had never realized. I stood up on the pedals and ignored the stabbing pain in my knees as the bicycle pushed forward. I could hear enthusiastic squeals and shouts of excitement behind me as Max and Mona let go of the handlebars. I felt the wind in my face as I glided down the road, pedaling madly and smiling on the back of my pistachio green stallion! I glanced back and saw Max and Coach Mona jumping with their hands in the air, while Shari preserved the whole voyage on film. Feeling a bit overwhelmed and out of control, I slammed on the brakes as Coach Mona ran beside me, making sure I did not fall. Neither of us could resist a smile as the bike came to a stop and I realized that a dream, which had begun nearly one year ago to the day, had finally come full circle! I'd actually ridden the pistachio green bicycle I had all but given up on. Granted, it had been a wild, wobbly ride with no athletic form or grace, but it was a beginning, a starting point—a place where determination found courage and together they created a miracle. It was also just hours before my actual birthday and a fitting way to end one journey just in time to begin another.

Lonely Days and Sleepless Nights

"The black cloud of devastation had first danced upon her head and shoulders and then, without any forewarning, it had pounced upon her, suffocating her entire being."

Standing silently with her hands clasped behind her back, Stella stood before the window, watching the raindrops splatter against the glass. The trees swayed as the wind whirled past and she jumped when a bolt of lightning forked across the sky, slicing through the steel-colored clouds as thunder rumbled and shook the foundation of her tiny home. Feeling a sudden chill, she wrapped the oversized, periwinkle-blue sweater a bit tighter around her ever shrinking body. As she quietly observed the elements pound away at the Earth outside, her heart pounded in eager anticipation of what lay just beyond the storm. Something told her the lost and lonesome life she had come to endure was about to change.

For nearly ten years, Stella had grown accustomed to the long, lonely days which melted into exasperating, sleepless nights. It had not been an easy decade to tolerate. In looking back, she could not recall how it all began or the spark which had ignited the inferno of destruction, but she *did* realize food had come to control her life. It was quite ironic how gaining so much weight had, in turn, caused her to lose so many other things. The black cloud of devastation had first danced upon her head and shoulders and then, without any forewarning, it had pounced upon her, suffocating her entire being. As she grew out of her clothes, hobbies, and friendships, she found herself immersed in a solitary existence where food was her closest companion. In an effort to numb the pain in her desolate heart, Stella submerged herself into an intensely intimate relationship with her refrigerator. The food, which had started off as a distraction, soon turned into a craving, a compulsion, and eventually, an addiction.

Last summer, upon reaching a sadness which was so extreme, she had considered taking her own life just to end the severe loneliness, she did not. Instead, Stella had chosen to wage war upon the monster who had stolen her existence. She studied and examined, investigated and explored all of the options she had at her disposal and then she developed a plan. Arming herself with everything she would need to do battle with this determined demon, she launched an attack which would ultimately transform her entire life. The past year had been filled with good food and good friends. "Healthy in and healthy out" had become her motto and she had remained steadfast when it came to exercise. This morning she had stepped onto the scale to a loss of two pounds this week. To some, that might sound trivial, insignificant, or trite; however, to Stella, the loss was enormous when tacked onto the ninety-nine pounds she had already lost over the past year. Yes indeed, in *her* mind, the battle had been won!

The ominous clouds tumbled away and the sun burned vibrantly in an effort to desiccate the soggy sky and as Stella watched in admiration, she knew in her heart it had become her time to shine, too.

Racing the Moon

"With cunning stealth, it crept upon her. One day, she was thriving and living life and the next, life began to proceed without her."

She drove through the day, aiming for the sun while running from the moon. Deciding to take a much needed mini vacation, she had stuffed a few things in an overnight bag and scrambled swiftly to her car. She had no real destination in mind, just this incessant need to keep moving, searching, fleeing... and so she did. Eventually, darkness dropped upon her and began to suffocate her momentum and still she drove. Speeding through the dead of night, her headlights cut through the blackness like a spoon through melting ice cream. While driving, she tried to remember when things had begun to change. She attempted to recall when all of the open doors began to close and all of those unlimited possibilities started to develop limits. With cunning stealth, it crept upon her. One day, she was thriving and living life and the next, life began to proceed without her.

As a young woman, she had been independent, strong, and beautiful. Often described as a pioneer in the vicious male-dominated circle of brokers controlling the Wall Street financial district, she was applauded for her steady head and remarkable foresight. Anything and everything was hers for the asking, or quite often, the taking. She could do no wrong because for her, simply making a wish meant making things happen. Quite possibly, her greatest mistake was in thinking it would last forever when everyone knows nothing ever does. Even rainbows fade and dreamers are saddened to find the heaping pot of gold they chased for so very long, holds but a few tarnished pennies.

There came a day when staying ahead of the game became a real challenge as she began slipping a bit and then swiftly fell behind. Without warning, her distractions became her obsessions. Each morning started off with a little white pill which allegedly took the edge off the forthcoming stressful day and the occasional glass of wine she enjoyed on special occasions turned into the evening bottle she consumed every night to help her sleep. Food became an addiction as she found herself stuffing something into her mouth from the moment she opened her eyes until she passed out watching television each evening. The excess weight began to smother her as it stole her confidence, self-assurance, and dignity. The bathroom scale, along with her entire expensive wardrobe, was boxed up and stacked in a darkened corner of the basement.

An overwhelming sadness took control of her once happy existence and the simple pleasures of life became dreaded apprehensions.

The shiny, black Lexus sped through the night with the moon in hot pursuit as its determined driver pushed forward in search of answers, resolutions, and solutions. As her conscience consulted her better judgement, she began to wonder if perhaps she should turn the car around and head toward home when suddenly, a notion entered her weary, exhausted mind. *What is home?* she wondered. Thinking for a moment, she decided home was meant to be a peaceful, cozy, safe, and inviting place that is shared with one's family. Quickly realizing her own residence reflected none of this, she let out an unexpected, agonizing sob, and then, just as suddenly, the tears began to slide down her cheeks. Rolling down her window, she hoped the cool night breeze might clear her mind and transform her melancholy mood. It did not. Turning up the radio, she began belting out "Against the Wind" with Bob Seger bitterly singing back up. Through the wind and the music and the moonlight, she realized the place she had left behind was not really her home at all. She began to wonder if perhaps her real home and family was waiting for her, somewhere out there past the blackness of this strange and unfamiliar night. It occurred to her that what was waiting behind her had not made her feel safe or happy and there was absolutely no family there anticipating her return. With that revelation, a lightbulb went off in her head... along with the low fuel light on her dashboard.

Pulling into a brightly lit Texaco gas station, she glided up next to the first available pump and refilled her exhausted gas tank. Walking inside to pay, the aroma of fresh, hot coffee filled her senses and enticed her to grab a cup. The first sip brought her back to life and she smiled as the warm java settled into her stomach. Upon turning to leave, she found herself standing directly in front of a wall of perfectly folded maps. Her eyes slid back and forth across the selection and settled upon a picture of a beautiful ocean sunrise on the cover of a North Carolina map. Instinctively, her hand reached for it and she carried it up to the older lady standing behind the counter. "Do you really suppose there could be a sunrise this beautiful out there in the world?" she asked, handing her a five dollar bill, not really expecting an answer. The woman paused, smiled, and said, with a twinkle in her eye, "Oh, it's out there, missy, but it's up to you to go and find it!" With that, she handed her the map and her change.

A huge smiled filled her face and she pushed her way through the glass door to discover she had driven an entire day and dawn was breaking. She stepped out into the parking lot and with a hammering heart, stared directly at the magnificence of a magenta-colored horizon splashed with blood red shards of approaching sunlight above the whitecap waves of what must be the Atlantic Ocean. She stared with awe and amazement and for the first time in her life, she felt like she was home.

The Results

"She sat alone in subdued silence and nearly fell apart when her name was finally called. With shaking knees, she pushed herself out of the chair."

Ellen opened her eyes just before dawn to what she imagined would be an ordinary day in her stale, boring, uneventful life. Wondering where the events of the day might lead, she tossed off the covers and bounced out of bed. The sudden commotion woke Ozzie, her sassy Yorkie, who began yipping in confused excitement. As the sun crept through the windows of her warm, comfy home, and the darkness of the morning sky burst into colorful shades of crimson and pumpkin, she began to feel a little something in the air. It was not anything she could wrap her mind around or put a finger on. It was nothing obvious, visible, or predictable, but there was something nonetheless. She stepped into her pink, fuzzy slippers and padded down the stairs with Ozzie racing behind her.

The scent of Swiss vanilla coffee filled the kitchen as Ellen poured a fresh, steaming cup from the pot. Holding the warm mug in her hands, she blew across the top, excited to taste that first sip, but not at the expense of scalding her tongue. Just as she'd gotten the nerve to take a drink, the phone sitting next to her burst into a frantic ring, causing her to jump and spill hot coffee all over herself. She glanced at her watch and noted the early hour of the phone call. She wondered who might be calling at eight a.m. with just a bit of hesitation, she sighed and lifted the receiver to her ear and with little more than a whisper, she said, "Hello?"

"Dr. Wilson's office," blurted a firm and assertive voice. "We have your test results," she stated coldly. Ellen's heart stopped as she inhaled sharply.

"Okay," she finally spoke into the phone. "And what did you find?" she asked, not entirely certain she was prepared to accept the answer she was about to receive.

"We don't discuss results over the phone, so we will need you to come back in for a consult with Dr. Wilson." Her heart sank into her stomach as the air escaped from her lungs and she dropped into the kitchen chair like a rag doll. "Hello? Hello?" came a concerned voice through the phone. "Are you alright?"

Ellen cleared her throat and answered with an unconvincing yes. She proceeded to write down the appointment time and date on a napkin sitting near her coffee cup and hung up the phone. She sat in silence, staring at the coffee-stained napkin, lost in thought as she remembered the day Dr. Wilson had given her the news which had both alarmed and terrified her. She'd spoken softly as she explained that Ellen's most recent pap results had come back abnormal and they would have to do a biopsy as soon as possible. Ellen had gone in two days later for the outpatient procedure and now, finally, the dreaded results were in. Her stomach churned and her mind began to race as she thought to herself, *Cancer… I have Cancer*. With Ozzie at her feet, she crossed her arms, sat back in her chair, and closed her eyes in an attempt to escape the dark and terrifying notions saturating her mind.

She wondered what would happen to Ozzie, the runt of his litter and loyal companion she'd raised since he was just a tiny pup. What about mom, who was still vibrant and healthy, but would one day need Ellen to care for her? What would happen to her stuff? The treasured things she had spent a lifetime accumulating which collectively revealed the story of her life. Suddenly, the "Whys" took over her thought process. *Why* had she waited so long to call the doctor? *Why* did she ignore the obvious symptoms? *Why* hadn't she eaten better or exercised more? Her mind began to throb with all of the *why, why, whys* banging around inside. She heaved a painful sigh as the tears tumbled uncontrollably from her eyes.

Over the next few days, she felt compelled to get her affairs in order. She buried herself in wills, insurance forms, past due bills, and paperwork. It made her feel organized and in control of a life which appeared to be spinning wildly out of control. It also helped to pass the time which crept by so slowly. Ellen began walking her little dog twice a day and even let him sleep on the pillow next to her in bed at night. The telephone remained pressed to her ear at night as she made calls to old friends, family, and past lovers. Mom was surprised when Ellen stopped by and treated her to a fancy dinner at her favorite Italian restaurant, where they talked, laughed, and reminisced until the manager finally locked the doors and turned off the bright neon "open" sign in the front window.

The following morning, Ellen stood in her kitchen beside the colorful lighthouse calendar on the wall. She found herself staring at the date in the center which had a bright red circle drawn around it: today's date. She glanced at her watch, snatched up the car keys, and headed out the front door to the dreaded doctor's appointment. There was a dark, definite chill in the air with clouds the color of charcoal circling madly overhead. Standing in the gusting wind, she found herself wondering if it were indeed cancer, would it take more courage to give up or to go on? Pausing a moment longer with her hair blowing in the wind, she finally slid into the car and drove swiftly down her street, blowing past two stop signs as she sped away.

While sitting in a very uncomfortable chair in Dr. Wilson's waiting room, Ellen's mind began to race once again and she felt a damp chill on the back of her neck. She sat alone in subdued silence and nearly fell apart when her name was finally called. With shaking knees, she pushed herself out of the chair. Ellen stumbled just a bit as she as she hurried through the door and past the nurse, into one of the small exam rooms. Stepping into the tiny room, her heart felt as cold as the stainless steel surrounding her. After an agonizing fifteen minutes, Dr. Wilson finally strolled into the room with clipboard in hand. She smiled a reassuring smile which brought Ellen a small sense of relief as she seated herself across from her and placed the clipboard in her lap. She looked into Ellen's searching eyes and said, quite simply, "Benign." Everything the doctor said after that was a blur; in fact, it seemed nothing more than a pile of words, pauses, and commas all strewn together into one long sentence, which meant absolutely nothing. That single word... benign... had freed her soul and given back her life.

Speechless, she stood and walked out of the sterile examination room and right out of the building. To her surprise, the hot July sun had melted the menacing clouds to reveal a gorgeous summer sky of turquoise blue and lavender. As she stepped into the sunshine, the world around her exploded from black and white into magnificent Technicolor! Tilting her head to the sky, she smiled as the rays of heat warmed her face and she realized she would never again take for granted the spectacular gift that was her life. Tonight, she would go home and eat macaroni and cheese out of the pan, drink milk out of the carton, and kiss Ozzie a dozen times.

Tonight, she would take a hot bath and then settle herself into the hammock hanging in the backyard. With not a single care in the world, she would lie there and enjoy the warm night air throbbing with bullfrogs and singing crickets where she would fall asleep with the stars winking above her in the remarkable evening sky.

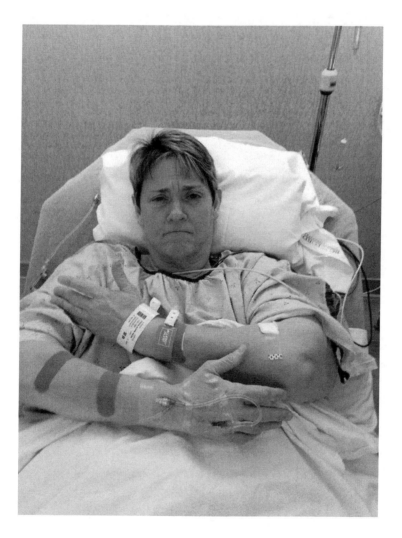

Unforeseen Disclosure

"Looming behind the inquisitive child, stood her mother, eyes wide open, with a mortified look on her face. Confounded, I swallowed hard and searched for the words to answer her candid enquiry."

While standing in line at the bank, holding my checkbook in one hand and my paycheck in the other, my thoughts and my gaze were directed toward the window and the approaching storm in the air. As I studied the cement gray sky and the ominous black clouds in the distance, I heard a small voice below me chirp, "Are you a boy or a girl?" Caught off guard, I abruptly jerked myself back inside the bank and looked down into the inquisitive blue eyes of a very young girl. Surprised by such candor from a child, I blurted out, "What did you say?" quite bemused. Responding quickly, she again reiterated her question, "Are you a boy or are you a girl?" as she placed her hands on her hips for a bit more emphasis.

Looming behind the inquisitive child, stood her mother, eyes wide open, with a mortified look on her face. Confounded, I swallowed hard and searched for the words to answer her candid enquiry. Before I could open my mouth, the teller called them up to the window and the girl's mother let out a definite sigh of relief as she yanked the child out of line and sprinted up to the counter. I exhaled, as well, feeling the blood drain from my cheeks as the other customers waiting for their turn at the window repressed their snickers.

When I got home that afternoon, I stood before the full-length mirror in my bedroom, staring at my reflection. The child's question played over and over in my head. "Are you a boy or a girl?" As I looked at myself, I could understand her bewilderment. With short hair cropped around my ears and resting upon the collar of a black polo shirt I had bought on clearance in the men's department of Macy's, my eyes traveled down the Levi jeans which scrunched up at the bottom to reveal the tops of my favorite tan, Timberland work boots. The rugged ensemble was topped off with a man's watch and a wallet in my back pocket. Yes, indeed, her confusion made perfect sense. My appearance was rather deceiving and I understood her query, for it was a question I had asked myself all of my life.

As a child, my boyish tendencies had been disregarded by family and teachers as a tomboy phase. Perfectly content playing with G.I.-Joe dolls and Tonka trucks, I passed off my Barbie dolls and Easy Bake Oven to my younger sister. There weren't any ballet, tap, or piano lessons for me after school. I spent my evenings playing basketball, baseball, and kickball with the neighborhood boys. Every year, I begged and pleaded for a Daisy pump action B.B. gun and smiled with glee when I finally received one on my thirteenth birthday. I spent many joyful Saturday afternoons shooting at tin cans and bottles in the back yard. In high school, the captain of the football team was of no interest to me. Instead, I spent my time at the games, sitting in front of the cheerleading squad with my elbows propped up on the bleacher behind me, watching the pretty girls over my high-top sneakers stretched out and crossed in front of me. I did not go to my senior prom because I refused to wear a dress, makeup, or high heels. Besides, no boy would have the nerve to ask me out for fear I would laugh at them or worse than that, I'd say yes!

"Are you a boy or a girl?" slipped back into my thoughts. What a profound and multifaceted question the little girl had raised. Had I been forced to give her an answer at that moment, there is no telling how I might have responded. As I turned to walk away from the non-judgmental reflection, I glance over my shoulder one last time and thought to myself, *I am not a girl, nor am I a boy.* I suppose I am just me, someone special in between.

Yesterday I Said Tomorrow

"So this is what giving up feels like. They say it happens to women of a certain age. Which leaves me wondering, What is the actual number which defines that age as certain and what is so certain about it?"

Yesterday I said tomorrow and tomorrow I will probably say the same. I've hit a rough patch. I seem to be stuck in a rut—wheels spinning wildly, yet going nowhere. Oh, I have been here before, looking for progress without any effort. The result is usually a day of pity, binging, overindulging, and overdoing followed by a night of regret, disappointment, and discontent. I think about starting over but I am not sure I have another fresh start or new beginning in me. The words seem hollow and echo inside of my head. I am sick and tired of the so called 'second chances' I find myself facing for the fiftieth time in my tenacious search for that elusive happy ending.

So this is what giving up feels like. They say it happens to women of a certain age. Which leaves me wondering, *What is the actual number which defines that age as certain and what is so certain about it?* I only ask because I may be standing on the threshold of that mysterious purgatory—that soft, tender, obscure spot right between middle and old age. The despairing women trapped in this position, fight it. First, by refusing to celebrate their birthdays. When asked about their age, they quickly respond with,

"How old do you think I am?" Holding their breath, they wait sullenly for an answer from the poor soul who has been put on the spot. One can see the extreme discomfort cross the queried person's face as their brain begins to frantically calculate and tally all of the clues and stockpiled information they have on said person. It is common courtesy to subtract five years from your calculation for good measure; after all, it may make the difference between silent satisfaction and suicide by massive cupcake consumption!

As I sit here alone, in a corner booth at the local coffee shop, writing in my journal, my mind drifts to my fast-approaching birthday. You know, that 'certain' one which puts me in the inescapable, transition position. My eyes scan the crowd of unusual characters in the room, finally settling on the glass pastry case at the front of the shop. The icing-drenched cinnamon buns and cream-filled cupcakes whisper my name as I fight the intense urge to go for my wallet and head toward the forbidden, frosted temptations. I consider the reality that today's diet has already taken a nosedive with the bacon I ate for breakfast, in addition to the peanut butter brownie I devoured after lunch, and I find myself inadvertently standing up. Inside of my head, I hear, "Well, what's stopping you?" while my heart murmurs, "Wait! No excuses... no regrets!" and I wonder if my head and my heart will ever end up co-existing on the same page! I realize that every single day I will be faced with choices. Some are hidden discreetly behind crafty temptations like the golden arches or a chocolate donut while others push you toward your discarded running shoes or a crispy, tossed salad. The ultimate decision must be made by each of us and the consequences dropped squarely upon our laps.

I sigh and grab my journal, sliding the pen behind my ear. The delightful scent of warm blueberry muffins cloud my mind as I walk past the tortuously, cunning showcase toward the front door. My feet fight with my legs to stop in front of the case but the muscles in my calves strain to drive me past and I feel a sense of relief as I step out into the warm sunshine.

Yesterday I said tomorrow…I think it's time I kept my word.

Alana Marie

The Reflection

"She walked back to the cunning mirror and stared at herself once again, when suddenly something struck like a bolt of lightning from an ominous sky."

Staring at her reflection in the mirror, she winced. The adverse adjectives which came to mind were less than flattering. Enormous, huge, and gigantic were just a few. With immense difficulty, she considered and examined the strange phenomenon she was faced with every single time she passed by this mirror. Over the past eighteen months, she had worked hard shedding over one hundred fifty pounds and yet her reflection remained the same. Day after day, she scrutinized her image in that dreary, insipid, full-length mirror, hoping to see a change. Although her family and friends praised her daily for her colossal weight loss, she could not see it.

She did, however, feel different. The knees which had hauled around those extra pounds for so many years were thankful for the relief, as were her feet. Even her heart felt stronger as it beat inside of her chest, and yet she still felt as though she weighed three hundred fifty pounds. That same heart still thrashed wildly when a waitress led her to a corner booth or her best friend offered her a free ticket to the Tiger baseball game. Seating is always a relentless source of anxiety for portly people who face snickers and whispers from judgmental onlookers as they attempt to squeeze into seats designed for others who are half their size. Not having faced such an experience recently, she smiled. Life had been a series of sliding easily in and out of questionable situations, and yet she continued to find herself filled with nervous apprehension at the thought of visiting new places and trying unfamiliar things. It was as though her three hundred fifty pound mind was trapped inside of her rapidly shrinking body. Plate glass windows still screamed derogatory obscenities as she strolled by. She imagined the children in the park whispering and making fun of her as she passed them, even though they appeared to be engrossed in their own jump rope skills and kickball competitions. The Big and Tall shop was still her clothing store of choice, although she now found herself drowning in the smallest size the store carried. Why, even today, the shirt she wore hung from her like a sheet on a clothesline.

She walked back to the cunning mirror and stared at herself once again, when suddenly something struck like a bolt of lightning from an ominous sky. The realization occurred that her massive girth had been a safety net for all these years, a reason to say no or to not go. In saying no, there was little risk of failure, ridicule, or embarrassment. Looking intently at the fifty-year-old face staring back at her in the looking glass, it struck her that she was fast approaching the winter of her years, and yet she found herself dizzy with the promise of one last spring in her lifelong journey. There was still plenty of sunshine and adventure ahead of her. She began to feel a sense of strength within, much like a crocus pushing itself up through the April soil, struggling to feel the warmth of the sun above. She began to blossom. Heading to the junk drawer in the kitchen, she grabbed a screwdriver and raced back to the hypercritical mirror and began removing the screws. Pulling the glass off the closet door, she decided she would not base her life on that reflection anymore. It was with great pride and satisfaction that she realized life was not about who you saw in the mirror every day, but instead, what you felt inside your heart... and her heart was bursting with the anticipation of a brand new adventure.

A Sense of Adventure

"She stared out of her window, watching the same yellow, uninspiring sun creep above the insipid horizon. The predictability of the routine sunrise filled her with a dreariness she could not seem to escape."

And there came a day when the life she had been living did not suit her anymore. The confined feeling of being ensnared in an unfulfilled existence consumed her thoughts. Everything in her sphere felt old and out-of-date. For a time—a *very* long time—her predictable world had given her a sense of safety and security. Now it only caused her to feel imprisoned and alone. In her heart, she longed for something fresh, uncommon, and unusual. She stared out of her window, watching the same yellow, uninspiring sun creep above the insipid horizon. The predictability of the routine sunrise filled her with a dreariness she could not seem to escape. Oh, how she longed for the exhilaration of seeing that orange ball of fire rise above the rippling waves of a turquoise blue ocean or emerge from behind a majestic, snow-capped mountain; and yet here she stood, day after day, thoughtlessly observing the same, unchanged vision of daybreak.

Notions of escape began to devour her thoughts. The restraints of her surroundings ultimately started to affect her mood and disposition, and there came a point where she thought she might actually go mad if she did not manage to find a way to liberate her soul. Long, weary nights were filled with separating and sorting while days centered on eliminating and removing the buried baggage of a disenchanted life. It suddenly occurred to her that holding on to these "things" was only keeping her down— holding her back. At this point, she began to purge wildly, resulting in her feeling lighter, happier, and stronger than she had in ages.

Then, one morning she awoke earlier than usual, feeling awkwardly anxious. The autumn winds were blowing. There was a chill in the air, filled with the promise of a brand new adventure. Her friends and family could feel it, too. Sensing her discontent, they kept their distance. Standing before her window, expecting the predictable, morning daybreak she had become accustomed to, she was quite astounded to bear witness to the most magnificent sunrise she had ever observed through this porthole. The blackness of the early morning sky proceeded to brighten as streaks of magenta and blood red began to seep into the clouds. As the sun climbed into the sky, it was as though a can of yellow paint had spilled into the existing red, causing the sky to explode into a kaleidoscope of fire. Staring, mesmerized by the beauty before her, she realized today was the day. Restlessness replaced complacency; anticipation pushed aside apprehension and the courage to take the first step of this imminent adventure became the focus of what would be the balance of her life. She left the window, pulled her worn leather suitcase from beneath her bed, and began packing knowing she would be gone before the first winter snowflake fell from the sky.

Every Last Bite

" Lauren had gorged herself into a coma last night—all week, in fact—telling herself, this was the final time... the last hurrah. After today, everything would change."

Lying in bed, Lauren pulled the pillow over her head in an effort to block out the annoying buzzing of her digital alarm clock. Suddenly realizing what day it was, she sat up and flipped the switch on the clock. Today was October 17, the day she had waited for, pleaded for and dreamed of for what seemed a lifetime. After fourteen years of being a prisoner—trapped inside of a body which stole and suffocated the life from her—today was the day she would be granted the keys to her freedom. Today, Lauren would surrender her body and her entire future to Dr. Matthews with hope that his miracle weight-loss surgery would change her miserable life. Many of her friends had looked down their noses at her, calling surgery 'the painless, easy way out,' but the decision to go under the knife had not been easy at all. Anything could happen, mistakes could be made, and even the excessive dose of anesthesia needed to knock her out and keep her under could potentially kill her. As for painless... well, the headaches, nausea, sugar hangovers, and strict diet were certainly not going to be a piece of cake and she did her best to block out the thoughts of massive hair loss and loose hanging skin. Nope, the direction she had chosen was so very far from easy.

Suddenly, an ominous wave of anxiety came over her as she rolled toward the edge of the bed. Lauren knew, in her heart, today's surgery was her last option. Nothing else had ever worked, and she had tried everything under the sun at least once… some twice! Sure, they produced slight results for a while and she lost a few pounds but when all was said and done, for every pound she had lost, she gained back three. All of these 'miraculous' diets had reneged on their promises, leaving her larger than life, struggling to survive at a whopping four hundred fifty pounds. As Lauren swung her enormous legs over the side of the bed and gradually stood up, she found herself already out of breath as her joints and bones popped and snapped back into place. She wobbled into the bathroom, squeezing her massive body into the small glass shower cube in an effort to get herself clean and ready for today's surgery.

Over the past few years, life had gotten so hard. Lauren was forced to leave a job she loved because standing on her feet all day had become impossible. She was thankful she'd managed to accrue a pretty large nest egg in her savings account, for it had sustained her over the past year and was going to pay for a significant portion of today's surgery. Her partner of more than seven years had also grown fed up with her vicious, unpleasant attitude. Tired of her negative outlook and emotional and verbal abuse, he'd gone for a ride one day and never came back. Friends and neighbors, who had grown weary of unanswered phone calls and doorbells, had ultimately given up trying to connect with Lauren. The only person she ever allowed into her ever shrinking world was her sister, Ava, who showed up once a week with bags of groceries and other essentials Lauren needed to survive. Ava had tried to help her sister eat healthier by adding fresh fruit and vegetables to every order. These items were never eaten and Lauren tossed them in the garbage right before Ava's next visit. She had been amazed at how Lauren continued to gain weight—even though she couldn't leave the house—and assumed Lauren was only eating the food she brought to her. What she *didn't* know was that Marco's Party Store and Pizza Place, located just around the corner, was more than happy to deliver all of her favorite food obsessions including pizza, subs, candy, chips and soda every couple days. In fact, they had just delivered Lauren's 'final supper' only yesterday. Knowing the surgery would end her ability to consume and enjoy all of her favorite food addictions, Lauren had gorged herself into a coma last night—all week, in fact—telling herself, this was the final time... the last hurrah. After today, everything would change. She knew this to be true because she had already Googled it. She had wondered if on 'special occasions' she would be allowed a piece of candy or two, or a hamburger or a Pepsi. The site had said that while it was not recommended, it was certainly 'possible.'

Lauren looked out the window and sat down at the kitchen table, waiting for Ava to arrive and drive her to the hospital. While sitting there, she eyed a Hershey bar, a leftover from yesterday's nine-hour 'pre-bypass' binge. Knowing she was not supposed to eat or drink before her surgery, she forced herself to look away. Eventually, her gaze fell back upon the shiny, brown wrapper. Picking it up, she felt a bit angry for missing it yesterday and cringed at the thought of throwing away a perfectly delicious candy bar. She stared at it as she headed for the garbage can in the corner of the room. As Lauren held it over the can, she found she could not let go and began to wonder if eating just a little bite would affect her surgery. *Probably not*, she rationalized as her fingers began to tear open the wrapper. Smelling the rich milk chocolate, she took just a small bite and closed her eyes as it began to melt in her mouth. The craving consumed her senses and before she could talk herself out of it, she began cramming the rest of the bar into her mouth, chewing furiously. As she swallowed the final bit of it, she realized with disgust that she should have not eaten it… but it would be absolutely the final, last candy bar of her life… wouldn't it?

Desperate Determination

" The weary rhythm of the clock seemed to match the desolate beat of her heart as the solemn days dissolved into empty nights, like vanilla ice cream melting in the sunshine."

She tried to remember when all of the open doors began to close, when unlimited possibilities began to discover limits. Thoughts turned to all of the I should have, I could have, and I would have moments, which had so covertly slipped through her fingers. She was unable to recall all the times she had uttered "I'll start tomorrow" as she'd pulled up to countless fast food drive-thru windows, ordering enough food for four people. It saddened her to think of all she might have accomplished over the past twenty years had she not squandered her entire existence. Staring out of her bedroom window as she lay sedentary beneath the blankets of her bed, she watched in silence as the black clouds rolled across the darkening skies of autumn. The barren trees swayed in the wind and she shivered with a sudden chill of unexplained dread and anticipation of the omen this squall had delivered to her door. The plastic alarm clock on the nightstand filled the room with a steady tick, tick, tick as the minutes of her lonely life slipped away from her. The weary rhythm of the clock seemed to match the desolate beat of her heart as the solemn days dissolved into empty nights, like vanilla ice cream melting in the sunshine. Her woeful brown eyes had rained ten thousand tears in her desperate desire for salvation and yet she remained helpless and hopeless, hidden away in her fortress, waiting in vain for someone… anyone to save her.

There came an unfortunate morning when she took a tumble rolling out of bed. Stepping down precariously onto the side of her foot, she'd twisted her ankle and crashed violently to the floor, pulling the little alarm clock, the lamp, and everything else that had accumulated on the cluttered nightstand down upon her. Dazed and dumbfounded, she scrambled wildly in an attempt to pull herself up off the floor. Feeling a sense of hopelessness, she began to hyperventilate which created a greater sense of nervous desperation. Twisting and turning madly on the carpet, she tried to maneuver her five-hundred-pound frame to a place where she could pull herself up; she could not. Instead, she lay there like a jellyfish on the shore as morning stretched into afternoon. With nothing else to do but think, she remained in the same spot, contemplating her current, dismal situation, her depressing life, and her dark, uncertain future. It occurred to her she had indeed reached the lowest, most vulnerable point in her miserable life. Alone and totally helpless, she realized all of the eating and cheating, the giving up and giving in, had brought her to this: her very own rock bottom in this revolting, isolated corner of hell. Sitting with her back against the wall—both literally and figuratively—she began to cry as she grasped the concept, that for once, she could not run away from this five-hundred-pound truth.

As the darkness of early evening began to paint the room a deep charcoal gray, a sense of anxiety wrapped itself around her as the possibility of her own demise filled her mind. Would all of her years of complacent life end here like this? Would her family find her lifeless body right next to her bed, covered in her own waste, muscles stiff with rigor mortis, ironically dead from starvation? The notion made her tremble and she felt, within her, a firestorm begin as she realized that after decades of waiting for someone to help her, she was indeed going to have to help herself.

With desperate determination, she rolled over to the edge of the king-sized bed, latched onto the frame, and began pushing herself up onto her bent, throbbing knees, which screamed in silent anguish. She let out a cry as she struggled to force herself into a standing position. The muscles in her calves bulged and her knees nearly buckled as sheer willpower pushed her massive body up off the floor. Panting and sweating, she toppled upon the bed. Her eyes welled with tears of hope and pride as she enjoyed this single moment of strength and power. It hit her like a boulder: the realization that she wanted to live. Not a day-to-day existence of basic survival but instead, she longed for a genuine life bursting with family, friends, learning, and romance! As her soul filled to the brim with this sudden desire to live, she became overwhelmed with enough courage to believe this time she would do it! For years she had wasted away in this lonely apartment, waiting for someone to save her. Tonight, she finally realized she could save herself.

To Say Goodbye

"It flooded her mind with so many unexpected emotions from envy to anger, and irritation to resentment, but mostly just sadness, as an overwhelming feeling of hopelessness began to fill her soul as their final days together slipped by."

Leaning with her back against the rough bark of the ancient oak, Sarah sat with her delicate hands resting in her lap. She relaxed in peaceful admiration of his rugged features and slender new body. What a handsome man he had become, but then again, she had always been attracted to him, even when his frame had been plump and pudgy. The magnetism she felt toward Kevin lay in his natural charm and steadfast dedication. These traits, combined with an effortless sense of humor and a genuine need to always do what was good and right, had compelled her heart to fall in love with him. The problem was, he did not know it and probably never would. He was leaving for college in just three short days and once he left, she knew he would never return.

Stretched out beneath the shade of the towering oak, Kevin relaxed with his fingers laced behind his head. His eyes were closed to block the glaring sunlight of what would surely be one of the last remaining days of summer. He was unaware she was observing him, watching with such love and tenderness, because he, in turn, was daydreaming about *her*, his lovely Sarah. Her flaxen hair and twinkling blue eyes had occupied his dreams for so many years. In his heart, he believed he had loved her always, and yet he had never told her so. Being overweight most of his life had crushed his confidence and stolen his potential. He had settled for her friendship because it was all he felt he deserved. Sarah was brilliant, beautiful, and perfect in every single way. She would never even entertain the idea of dating a flabby frump like himself when she could have anyone she desired… absolutely anyone.

For the past year, Sarah had watched in awe as Kevin ran and trained and transformed his squishy body into a sleeker, stronger, healthier version of his former self. To her, he'd been perfect all along with the courage of a warrior and the patience of a saint. He'd been her knight in shining armor for as long as she could remember. Throughout middle school, the classroom bullies had tormented Sarah for being too skinny. The name Olive Oil had been carved into her locker and remained her unofficial nickname until she gleefully transferred to high school in 2011. Middle school had caused her to feel hideous and ugly, which explains why she could never tell Kevin how she felt about him. Sarah believed he deserved so much more than she could offer, and so the secret remained locked away inside of her aching heart.

Opening his eyes, Kevin caught her staring. Quickly, Sarah looked away and a smile spread across her face. Now it was his turn to gaze at her in awe and silent admiration. In just a few short days, he would pack his old Chevy and head off down the interstate to Eastern University, where he would spend the next four years of his life immersed in his studies. During the past few weeks, his dreams had often ended in his driving away with Sarah's face in his rearview mirror, smiling at him, until it would disappear and become just a memory of what might have been. With no self-confidence or hope for a future with Sarah, he was content to just be near her, to make her smile and hear her laugh. Oh, how he loved her laugh! As his eyes caressed her porcelain white skin, he wondered with a very heavy heart, just how would he exist without his Sarah?

As Kevin's body changed, other girls began to take notice. He pretended not to observe their batting eyes and flirtatious ways, but Sarah noticed. It flooded her mind with so many unexpected emotions from envy to anger, and irritation to resentment, but mostly just sadness, as an overwhelming feeling of hopelessness began to fill her soul as their final days together slipped by. Eventually, the day arrived when Sarah found herself standing beside Kevin as he shoved the last box of clothes into his jam-packed car. The storm clouds rolled across the sky as he slammed the trunk with a thud and somberly turned to face Sarah. His heart was pounding with both dread and anticipation. He could still tell her. It was not too late. His trembling hands reached out for hers and he stared deep into her puzzled, apprehensive eyes as the black clouds opened up and the raindrops began to fall.

Sarah fought back the tears as Kevin's hands closed around her own. Looking up, her gaze fell upon his milky brown eyes and they stood there in the driving rain, neither one daring to speak the words that would forever change the direction their lives. Instead, they remained standing silently, so close she could have kissed him and yet she stood motionless, petrified, and frozen in time. Sarah felt very thankful for the rain which diluted the tear drops that plummeted from her eyes. Gradually, Kevin's grip lessened and eventually, their hands gently fell apart. He looked away, searching for the words while her emotions spun out of control, and yet their silence was thunderous... nearly deafening. Finally, unable to actually utter the words 'goodbye' or 'farewell,' he turned and slid into the front seat of the idling car. Backing out of the driveway, he shifted into drive and drove desolately down the street. Kevin glanced into his rearview mirror to see Sarah standing in the pouring rain, arms crossed and her head down. As she disappeared behind him, he thought to himself, *Endings come too fast and goodbyes far too soon,* but the regret he felt in his heart would undoubtedly last forever.

Silent Addiction

"Your adversary has the potential to attack in many forms, but make no mistake; this is as close to meeting the devil as you will ever come."

Understand this: you never really see it begin. It starts somewhere in your existence when you are at your weakest. Stress is undoubtedly high while spirits are unquestionably low. Feeling alone, trapped in a life which is probably spinning out of control, you search in desperation for something, *anything*, you can take charge of and regulate. Subconsciously, you come to realize, that while you don't always have power over what happens *outside* of your body, you *do* have control over what goes *into* it. And so it begins.

Some people take great pains in choosing their weapon of self-destruction, and sometimes the menace chooses you. Either way, this unanticipated affiliation has the power to devastate and ruin your entire life. The ironic piece of this peculiar puzzle is the curious manner in which the bad habit you started—in an attempt to obtain some semblance of control in your life—ultimately takes control of you. When this unexpected shift happens, there will be no pity or compassion because you suddenly find yourself in a struggle for your life with an unrelenting, merciless opponent. It will start slowly, gradually, but very deliberately. The cocktail or pain killer you take to relax on the weekend inadvertently becomes a craving on Tuesday night. The healthy food that once filled your shopping cart has been replaced by cookies, candy, and frozen pizza. As your infatuation with your newfound distraction increases, so does your silent addiction.

The elusive changes will occur in gradual degrees, so don't expect to notice... you won't. The indulgences you previously enjoyed in pleasant social settings quietly become private obsessions, hidden compulsions, and an uncontrollable hunger. The sudden impulse to feed your selfish desires will increase as your ability to ignore it decreases. The foundation of your life will begin to crumble as your hopes and dreams disintegrate. There will come a day when it will seem your addiction has won. Your adversary has the potential to attack in many forms, but make no mistake; this is as close to meeting the devil as you will ever come. The demon will drop you to your knees and you will ultimately be forced to choose between forfeit and fight, life and death. The weaker sorts will relinquish their souls to the assassin, while others will unearth powers of strength and fortitude. Propelled by an intense determination to survive, they will find the ambition and strength to pick up the shattered pieces of their lives and begin again. These are the survivors. These are the champions.

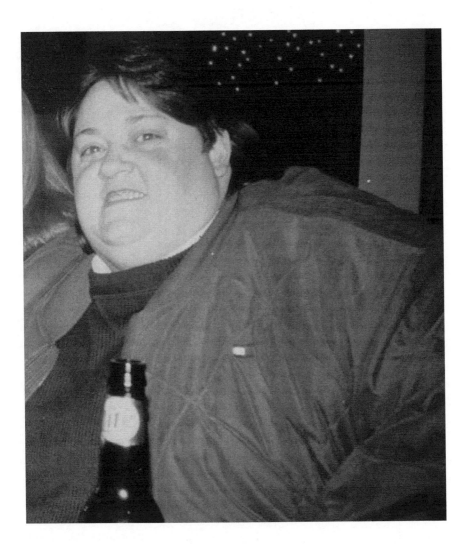

To Hold On

.

"Friends and family pretended not to notice I'd given up on all of my hopes, dreams, and ambitions. What they did not realize was I had actually given up on life."

Sometimes it takes more courage to walk away than to stay. It's the holding on that will kill you. The extra weight that keeps you down and holds you back from living the adventurous life your soul yearns for. You attach yourself to a job you hate that pays the bills, or a man who does the same. You spend far too much time convincing yourself you have no other options while making the best of the hand you've been dealt. I understand this phenomenon for I have lived it.

So many precious years were lost as I sat trapped inside of a five-hundred-pound body, while the world outside went on without me. Friends and family pretended not to notice I'd given up on all of my hopes, dreams, and ambitions. What they did not realize was I had actually given up on life. Surrendering to my food addiction nearly killed me while the loneliness I experienced consumed my every waking moment. Not a single genuine smile graced my lips for nearly a decade as I sat alone, waiting for someone or something to save me. Without hope, it becomes so easy to give up as the struggle of just holding on overtakes the excitement of actually living. There came a day when my hands were numb, battered, and blistered from battling to just hang on, that I faced the option to let go. It was a day when the fear of living became greater than the fear of dying. Life is about seeing, hearing, and experiencing new things. Happiness comes from the smiles, joy, and laughter of others combined with our daily relationships and the interactions we enjoy, with our family and friends. Isolation is devastating and debilitating, and I was surrounded by the emptiness of it every day and night.

And then it happened. I awoke one morning with the sun, feeling a supernatural strength and fortitude within me. It pumped up my heart and reignited the embers inside my soul. My mind began to crave new things and fresh adventures. As I stood up from the bed, my tired, twisted legs throbbed with pain, yet I ached to feel the muscles in my thighs and calves work again. It was as if my mind, body, and soul had made a pact to insure my survival, working together to bring my nearly dead body back to life. The process was prolonged and difficult. There were days when I longed to quit, but as time passed, so did these self-defeating thoughts. Today, two-hundred-fifty pounds lighter, I am thankful for the courage which found me, the determination which carried me, and the happiness which has consumed me. Every day gets just a bit easier and my life a little bit better. It's been a tough journey, but I realize there is just no shortcut to a comeback, so it only makes sense to enjoy the ride!

Counting the Days

"Was there anything left to look forward to? Was it too late to dream, hope, or even plan the final season of my life? "

I had reached a point in my life where I found myself female, fat, and fifty. Feeling deflated as I looked at my life thus far, I began counting the days left ahead in an effort to forget those behind me. Tired of pondering all the things I hadn't done in my lifetime and the magnificent dreams I had only achieved in my sleep, I began to feel a bit melancholy. I could clearly remember the glorious days of my youth—the awards, the scholarships, the good friends, and my first love. It was also easy to recall the mistakes of the past few years—the weight gain, the drinking, the break-up, and the loneliness, but there was a large part of living which had gone missing in between.

I stood at the window, staring at the huge maple tree in the center of my yard, and watched the leaves change colors before my eyes. The autumn wind puffed and panted, driving them from their branches and sending them spinning madly down to the earth below. I imagined myself as one of those falling leaves, spiraling frantically out of control. Like the sturdy maple, I had enjoyed the bloom and flourish brought on by the warm rains of springtime. The summer sunshine had warmed my entire soul, helping me grow and blossom into a unique and beautiful individual, ready to thrive and accomplish great things in the world. However, the crispy autumn winds had crept so unexpectedly upon me and halted my growth and progress, leaving me here twisting in the wind, incredibly alone, and dreadfully afraid.

What would become of me now? I wondered. Was there anything left to look forward to? Was it too late to dream, hope, or even plan the final season of my life? Fifty years old, after all, seems ancient in the eyes of many. In all actuality, going on would be more like starting over since I had nothing of value to call my own. I had driven away my lover, squandered all of my money, and snubbed most of my friends. My business was failing and there was no hope of another career in sight. The final point of concern was my health, which in all honesty, might be the greatest nightmare of all. Without a doubt I ate too much. This was evident every time I peeked into my walk-in closet filled with expensive clothes that would not button anymore. The empty bottles of wine stashed in my garage and under my sink exposed another bad habit I had developed during my mid-life crisis. The alcohol and food binging, combined with the sleeping pills I needed to put my stress to sleep at night, all added up to a heart attack just waiting to transpire.

Feeling quite beleaguered, I strolled into my sitting room, tossed a log on the hearth, and proceeded to light a warm, comforting fire. Sitting alone in resounding silence, a sensation of peace and tranquility came over me and I began to dream, an extravagance in which I had not allowed myself to indulge for quite some time. I thought about my lonesome, solitary life as the fire crackled beside me and my head filled with words, phrases, and ideas. Eventually, my mind became so full that the words began crashing into one another. Pushing myself up and out of my old leather chair, I stumbled to my great-grandfather's roll top desk, where I rummaged around for an old and worn diary which had not been seen in at least a dozen years. The soft-covered journal felt soothing in my hand as I reclaimed my warm seat by the fire. It wasn't long before I began to write. The words cascaded onto the page like April rain tumbling from the sky. Quietly, I wrote and recorded for hours upon endless hours and only ceased writing when a chill filled the room as the embers in the fireplace finally winked out. Glancing out the window, I observed thousands of silent stars twinkling in the pitch black sky and yawned as I turned to stare at the countless pages which had been filled in just one short night. Perhaps life hadn't closed its doors on me yet. Maybe I actually had something special left to offer others in the way of words, advice, and life lessons. Standing and stretching my arms above my head, a yawn escaped my chest as intense exhaustion finally hit me. Smiling with satisfaction, I tenderly placed the sleepy journal on the coffee table and headed up the stairs to my bedroom with a true sense of purpose combined with the undeniable realization that a pill would not be necessary to fall asleep tonight.

Believe

"The young have forever while the aged cherish moments, realizing tomorrow is not guaranteed. "

The universe works in an enchanted, magical manner. It takes great gratification in calling out 'abracadabra' at the most unexpected moments. Despite the sudden shock and surprise, the magic lies in the inspiration and motivation it can stimulate within a person who is on the verge of subtle surrender. I had reached that point. The adventure had become tiresome and tedious and I, the captain, had become so preoccupied in the voyage that I had lost focus of the destination. In all honesty, the twenty-year voyage I'd traveled had, in truth, been more like a roller coaster ride of wild and crazy highs and devastating lows, with me crashing to rock bottom more times than I care to remember. With the passing of time, the hills became so much more difficult to climb. The young have forever while the aged cherish moments, realizing tomorrow is not guaranteed.

In years past, I had lived my life believing in the assurance that things had to get better. With all of my faith and belief in that promise, I would lay my head upon my pillow every night to sleep and dream of freedom. For some, freedom is financial while for others, it involves matters of the heart. For me, it meant just being normal, average, and ordinary. Sounds like a modest request, one of low aspiration, doesn't it? I dreamed of waking up on an autumn afternoon to take a simple walk through the park and hear the brittle leaves crunch beneath my feet as I listened for the Canadian geese overhead, flying south for the winter.

Through my hopeless years of morbid obesity, I lived each day looking forward to crawling into bed at night, to fantasies of dancing and running, of traveling and love. These sweet dreams became my reality, just as the moon became my best friend. Little did I know, the universe had provided me with those visions to encourage and entice, within my soul, a longing for a life which would ensure my future. There came a night—when I was lost in contented dreams—that my mind and my body plotted an intervention and without my consent, launched a plan to save my life. I awoke the next morning feeling unusual, intense, motivated, and strong. Thus began an unexpected odyssey which would lead me to this particular place in time.

Today, as I look at the calendar upon my wall, I see I am just ten days short of my fifty-fifth birthday, one that is indeed a milestone in my life. The reality I am still alive is a miracle I appreciate with immeasurable respect and reverence. My five hundred twenty-eight pound body could have given up and shut down decades ago and yet it has endured to grant me one more abracadabra moment. Climbing upon the scale, watching the digital screen blink and flicker, I am astounded to see a number that has not appeared in quite a while. Surprised, I step off and let the scale go back and recalculate; however, when it does, I see the same number shining back at me. It says two hundred seventy-seven pounds, which is, in fact, the lowest number I have seen in nearly thirty years. Now, while this number may not be earth shattering to most, and an annoying, unwelcome number to many, it is a victory for me. It instills within my heart the hope, strength, and courage to continue on this unpredictable adventure. Tomorrow, the scale may bounce back up a pound or two, but today I celebrate a triumph as I tip my hat to the universe and realize I *do* believe in magic!

Pick a Season Cupcake!

Winter

A Christmas Blessing

"The image caused her to reflect on days gone by when she, too, had felt suffocated, smothered, and repressed. It seemed inconceivable that only three short years ago she had given up on life."

Sitting there in subtle silence, she stared through the frosted glass, rocking quietly and contently as the snowflakes tumbled from the sky. The wind blew and they began to pile up outside around her little country cottage. The white drifts blanketed the yard, seeming to suffocate the earth and all that lay beneath. The image caused her to reflect on days gone by when she, too, had felt suffocated, smothered, and repressed. It seemed inconceivable that only three short years ago she had given up on life. Weighing well over five hundred pounds, feeling as though every Christmas might be her last, the holidays brought overwhelming sadness with them.

Glancing around the room in full awe and appreciation of the crackling fire, her mother's handmade wreath on the door and the twinkling pine tree in the corner, she could remember a Christmas that was not so charming and perfect. With profound melancholy, she recalled sitting abandoned and alone in her little one-bedroom apartment, an empty can of ravioli on the counter and a single Christmas card from her mother standing upon the television set. Wincing at the thought of her massive bulk wedged tightly inside of her groaning easy chair, she remembered the utter hopelessness she had felt and the lonesome existence she had been forced to accept. The isolation and solitude were the hardest things to endure, and she had longed for someone, *anyone*, to talk to, to laugh with, and to love. The stillness of her home was overwhelming at times, causing her to wonder if she might, one day, die of a broken heart. The days between Thanksgiving and New Year's Eve all seemed to fuse together with her sleeping as much as fourteen hours a day just trying to get through them. With no family, presents, or Christmas spirit, there was absolutely nothing 'happy' about the holidays for her.

Three years ago, on New Year's Eve, she watched the ball drop in Times Square on her nineteen-inch television set. As the confetti fell from the sky and the crowds of people hugged, laughed, cheered, and danced, she sat alone and made a wish, a vow, or maybe a resolution. Praying for something better, she launched a request out into the universe, yearning for just one more chance at happiness—just a single opportunity to turn her life around. Feeling dizzy for a moment, she rested in total stillness and then, suddenly, a barrage of tears began to rain from her eyes. An endless torrent of long, buried frustration and sadness surged from her body and she began to feel free. An unexpected sense of hope, courage, and possibility emerged and with that single wish came the bravery she needed to turn her life around.

Today, experiencing a brand new healthy life at half the size she had been, she took the time to count her blessings, and there were many. Gazing into the fireplace, she watched the flames dance and smiled as the wood crackled and popped. At that moment, her companion, lover, and best friend stepped into the room, smiling, carrying two cups of steaming hot peppermint cocoa and she rejoiced in the magnificent gift of second chances.

The Package

"My heart beat wildly as I reached into the bottom of the broken cardboard box and placed my hand upon a book—a plain and simple book which held the stories of my life."

As my car swung into the driveway, I noticed a plain and unpretentious package sitting idly on my porch, covered with a dusting of snow. Bending over, I brushed it off, picked it up, and carried it into my cozy little home while searching for a return address. My breath caught in my throat as I spotted it. Setting the box on my dining room table, I peeled open the lid as the sound of the stiff, clear packing tape crackled and snapped beneath my fingers. I opened the little box slowly, with great anticipation, as one might open a newly found treasure chest reclaimed from the bottom of the ocean. My heart beat wildly as I reached into the bottom of the broken cardboard box and placed my hand upon a book—a plain and simple book which held the stories of my life.

The cover was cool and smooth and slid easily into my hand. Slowly, I lifted it out and into the light while my face felt flushed and my hand shook just a bit. As I slipped my fingers inside the cover and touched the first page, it hit me that my lifelong dream had indeed become a reality and with the first word of that opening chapter came the closing of another. Within the pages were the lonely days of weighing nearly a quarter of a ton along with the endless nights of drunken madness which eventually bled into late afternoon hangovers. Staring at the words, I was reminded of the wasted days and nights squandered while living a life of dangerous excess.

The book itself was a chronicle of my existence, holding together all of my pain and anguish in one neat little package for the whole world to read, critique, and criticize. My life was now, quite literally, an open book. Standing there in the quiet shadows of my home, I felt extremely isolated and alone. After a few moments of quiet reflection, I began to realize maybe I was not. I recognized other people like myself—the lost, lonely, and forgotten—might stumble upon this pint-sized treasure chest of emotion and maybe, just maybe, they would gather a bit of hope. Perhaps they, too, might find the courage and bravery to do battle with the demons controlling their lives. Through my stories they might find the inspiration to try, yet one more time, to rid their lives of the physical and emotional baggage they perpetually carried upon their backs.

Suddenly, it seemed okay to bare my soul and share the deepest, darkest secrets of my past. If my heartache could help guide just *one* person out of the darkness of their addictions, then the sharing of those secrets would be well worth the sacrifice. With that thought warming my heart, I carried the book to my caramel-colored easy chair, lit a fire, and opened it to the first page and began reading the story of my life.

Without Warning

"Suddenly, there came a knock on the front door which startled Rachel. Her breath caught in her chest as she stared at it in stark terror."

Rachel winced as she bent to pull the plastic makeup case from the very back of the bathroom closet, where it had been sitting since the last cover-up conspiracy. Her back and ribs ached as she lifted the case off the floor and set it upon the vanity counter. Keeping her head down, she did her best to avoid eye contact with her own reflection in the mirror as she carefully popped open the latch and began setting the little containers of cover-up, foundation, and makeup in a neat row across the counter. She sighed as she realized, in anguish, that this occasional practice had become a dreaded routine.

Rachel let her mind drift to a sweeter place and time—a cold winter afternoon, just a few short years ago, when she'd been a struggling college student, studying for finals at the university coffee shop. Fatigued, she had found herself staring through the glass door, daydreaming, when suddenly it opened with a loud groan. Wind and snow blew in through the door, bringing with it a tall, handsome stranger packaged quite attractively in a navy blue woolen coat accented with a long, red winter scarf slung around his neck, dancing in the wind behind him. Rachel's heart had skipped a beat as he rushed through the door. Taking notice of his jet black hair and dancing green eyes, she watched his every move as he made his way to the counter, where he placed his order and flirted shamelessly with the giggling barista. While waiting for his order, he turned, crossed his arms, and leaned casually against the counter, scanning the room inquisitively. It was at that very moment Duncan's eyes discovered Rachel's and forever changed the direction of her life.

She lifted her head to finally acknowledge the desolate reflection waiting impatiently for her in the mirror. The face she observed staring back at her demanded respect, recognition, and accountability, yet all she felt was disappointment and pity. Her right eye had all but swollen shut during the night despite the icepack she had balanced on her throbbing face while she pretended to sleep. The whole side of her face was painted black and blue and bloated while her front tooth felt loose to the touch. The broken image in the mirror made it clear that no amount of makeup could conceal the damage he'd inflicted this time, and she released a heavy sigh as she picked up her cellphone to message her supervisor, Katie. It sickened her to think she would have to call in sick yet another day and probably three. Katie, for the most part, had been pretty understanding, mostly because they had become friends while working together on a daily basis for more than a year. Last month, however, after several verbal notices, she'd been forced to issue a written warning and this absence would probably be the final straw. Oh well, she thought, I'll find another job, but her heart ached as she set the phone down on the counter.

*****

Sitting in her office, Katie's iPhone began to vibrate and her heart sank as she read the message from Rachel on the screen. She had felt trapped in this situation, trying to be understanding for her friend yet still fulfilling her obligations to the company. She watched and comprehended the messy situation between Rachel and her husband, Duncan, yet was not comfortable addressing it, mostly because she did not want to force Rachel to confess her embarrassing situation. She had, instead, nodded in sympathy while Rachel relayed her feeble stories about falling down the stairs, bumping her head, or minor fender benders on the highway. Katie bit her tongue in disgust and anger, knowing it was not her place—as a supervisor, anyway—to pressure Rachel for the details of her private life. In all reality, everyone in the office knew the cold, hard truth and gossiped about her when she left the room, yet no one ever said a word to Rachel. Katie stood up, walked over to the window, and stared out over the parking lot, trying to ignore the dreadful feeling which had so suddenly enveloped her.

*****

Wandering aimlessly through the house, Rachel thought to herself, Perhaps it's time to explore other options, and then began laughing out loud at this idea of "options," knowing that in all reality, she had none. If she left, Duncan would find her—just as he had several times before—and proceed to sweet talk her into coming home, again. If she stayed, hoping for change, she knew it was only a matter of time before Duncan had one of his drunken meltdowns and she would, again, end up at this same place—

licking her wounds, just thankful to be alive. For a moment, she entertained the thought of leaving. Even if she could muster up the courage to pack and run, she had absolutely no place to go. Family and friends who had helped her in the past, only to see her go back to this madman, had all but given up on her. They could not understand and were frustrated with Rachel's intense devotion to this monster who was intent on making her life a living hell. Rachel let out a sigh, accepting the realization that this was the hand she'd been dealt, and like it or not, she had no other options left. Looking at her watch, she decided she'd best get the house cleaned and dinner in the oven before Duncan came home; he'd be in a better mood today. Limping into the kitchen she got the red vase out from under the sink, knowing he would walk meekly through the door after work with a beautiful bouquet of flowers and an apology just for her.

Suddenly, there came a knock on the front door which startled Rachel. Her breath caught in her chest as she stared at it in stark terror. Shaking her head, she laughed nervously to herself, realizing Duncan would never knock on his own door. However, this led to the question of who would actually be on her porch at this early hour. Well, whoever it was could not see her in such a state. She walked toward the kitchen, hoping the intruder would just go away, at which point, the polite knocking turned into persistent pounding. Annoyed, Rachel made her way back down the hallway to the entryway. Taking a deep breath, she asked hesitantly, "Who is it? Who's there?"

A faint, familiar voice forced its way beneath the heavy oak door. "It's me... Katie," announced the caller. "Please open the door." Frustrated and feeling exposed, Rachel panicked, not wanting anyone—especially her boss—to see her like this. "Rachel, I know what's going on and I want to help," announced the warm voice. Feeling cornered and defeated, she fumbled with the lock and slowly twisted the doorknob. Katie gasped in alarm at the initial sight of Rachel's bruised and beaten face. Reaching out, she grabbed her hands and then embraced her in a comforting hug. Feeling safe for the first time in such a long while, Rachel's eyes welled up with tears and she sobbed violently as they streamed down across the purple bruises on her battered face. They stood there in the doorway for what seemed an eternity and finally, as the sobbing subsided, Katie lifted Rachel's solemn face, looked her in the eyes, and said simply, "Let's get packed." In contented silence, Rachel grabbed Katie's hand and stepped out onto the porch and into the summer sunshine, stating simply and securely, "Let's go. I don't need a damn thing!"

A Lonesome Christmas Eve

"It was a wall I had built around myself to keep the pain out and my emotions in. The walls increased, day by day, brick by brick, until it was so lofty I felt I might smother myself."

It is Christmas Eve and I sit here, alone, to dwell upon the mistakes of my past. Sadly, I consider the lost and lonely years wasted inside of a massive body which served as my protector from the outside world. It was a wall I had built around myself to keep the pain out and my emotions in. The walls increased, day by day, brick by brick, until it was so lofty I felt I might smother myself. I sat inside the prison I had created for myself for nearly twenty years, until I finally found the courage to seek help. Bravery guided my journey to freedom, and that, along with steadfast determination, paved the way to my subsequent liberty and independence.

Tonight, I sit here, physically half the person I once was, yet spiritually twice the person I used to be. The stillness of the night is deafening yet so perfect for reflection and meditation. I shake off the lonesomeness which envelopes me and begin to count my blessings.

Let the snow fall from the sky like tropical rain... I will be safe and warm in my cozy little home, in front of the fireplace, wrapped in a thick, red blanket. Tonight, I will read and write and drink hot cocoa with miniature marshmallows, enjoying what will most likely be the first snowstorm of the season. My puppies will surround me, thankful for the unexpected evening they will spend sleeping on my lap. I could complain but I won't. I could be angry that my Christmas Eve was spoiled because I am alone, but I will not. Instead, I will breathe and pull open all of my drapes and curtains, allowing myself to be hypnotized by the brightness of a giant silver dollar moon. In great serenity, I will watch the snowflakes pile up and cover all that is ugly. A power much greater than I can imagine has decided I need this time to myself— a day to slow down, relax, and reflect on all things good. And that is what I will do. I will lose myself in words, music, snowflakes, and marshmallows. What was meant for today can wait until tomorrow. A bit of silence is good for the soul.

The Power of Christmas

"As she observed herself, she stared into her own pleading eyes.

Eyes that screamed, "Don't give up. Fight, damn it, fight!"

Bent over the shovel in her driveway on Christmas morning, she huffed and puffed as she struggled to clear a path to her old, gray Chevy. Her coat, which barely covered her hulking figure, would not close anymore and made this task a very frigid one. Exhausted after just a few minutes, she decided to leave this job until tomorrow when the sun was due to shine. Looking down the street and watching the neighborhood children play, she recalled how she, as a young girl, had so loved the blustery, white days of December—snow angels in the front yard and even better, snowballs aimed at unsuspecting boys pulling sleds down the street. She remembered snowflakes in her hair and melting on her tongue and creamy hot chocolate waiting for her when she finally came inside with a red nose and frozen fingers. She would run up the stairs and into the warm, cozy house, slamming the door hard and leaving the Christmas wreath lying upon the front porch behind her.

On Christmas Eve, her mother would hustle and bustle around the kitchen, preparing the traditional holiday meal. The house would swell with the smells of roasting turkey, yams, and Dutch apple pie. Her family would stuff themselves and then retire to the sitting room where they would rest in front of a roaring fire, retelling holiday stories of days gone by while listening intently for any signs of Santa in the sky above. Eventually, she would fall asleep on the floor only to awaken before dawn on Christmas day, somehow snugly tucked into her own bed. With eyes blinking open, she would spring out of bed, running excitedly down the stairs and straight to the front room where the majestic tree stood proud and strong, twinkling in all its glory. Surrounding it would be colorful packages of every shape and size, decorated with sparkling bows, bells, and ribbons. Her breathing would stop as she stood mesmerized, staring with awe and amazement. After a moment of the purest silence, she would let out a howl so loud it woke the entire house! The family would gather, tired and bleary eyed, around the tree and they would ohhh and ahhhh while tearing the beautiful wrapping paper off all of the presents.

Those were rich days indeed, filled with golden memories which would last a lifetime. Today, however, she walked back into the quiet house, alone. There was no tree or turkey on this

Christmas morning, nor carols or glowing fire. She lumbered into the bedroom where she paused to look at herself in the mirror. She stared at her swollen face and bloated body and decided she rather resembled a snowman standing there. Her clothes were stretched to extreme limits, with buttons straining and ready to pop. She let out a huge sigh and turned her head quickly in shame. *When had this transformation happened?* she wondered in complete sadness. It was at this precise moment she woefully realized she had given up. She had not only given up on herself but she had also given up on life. She had lost her innocent zest for adventure. The simple happiness of her youth was gone. It became an effort to even fake a smile. She forced herself to look back into the mirror again and saw the beseeching eyes, lost deep inside the flesh of her face, disappearing like a candle flame being smothered in its own melting wax. As she observed herself, she stared into her own pleading eyes. Eyes that screamed, "Don't give up. Fight, damn it... fight!" In that moment, her heart began to beat faster and harder as she straightened her back and eyed herself unhappily. She thought she felt something snap inside of her, much like a kernel of popcorn in a hot pan or the tight bud of a rose which has finally reached its bloom. Feeling a spark of fire inside, she began to feel alive. There was a renovation of epic proportion taking place within her soul. Perhaps it was a Christmas gift of sorts, a package filled with hope, strength, and promise. She could not decide what it was, but only that it was happening. She realized the road back would not be an easy one—full of twists and turns, even dead ends—but she knew she was ready. With steadfast faith and determination, she took a deep breath, a last look in the mirror, and spun on her heel to take the first step of what would be a very long journey. She had faith she could do it even if she could only manage to do it one step at a time.

To Begin Again

"She had dreamt of birthdays, school days, and holidays. Yes, dreams can be wonderful, but life can be cruel."

She sat silently with her hands on the steering wheel and her head leaning against the seat, staring aimlessly at the sun creeping over the edge of the vast, empty parking lot. It painted the horizon in a breathtaking array of purple and red and for a moment, she felt the calm serenity of a brand new day. The only sound she could hear was the steady vibration of her keys in the ignition. Eventually, she reached out and turned the car off, stashing the wad of keys into her jacket pocket. Emitting a great sigh, she pushed open the car door and stepped out into the cool morning breeze. She spotted an empty shopping cart beside her car and decided to grab on to it for support. She was feeling a bit shaky today.

Walking through the big double doors, she strolled past the senior greeter standing at the entrance. The old woman flashed a smile, which was unexpectedly missing a front tooth, and offered a sale paper and a pleasant good morning. She nodded and kept walking past, ignoring the outstretched hand holding the wrinkled newspaper. She was thankful to see the empty aisles since she was in no mood to deal with crazy coupon clippers or dawdling grandmothers. She rolled up and down the rows of colorful merchandise, pausing for a moment to investigate a rack of clothes marked 'Clearance.' It filled her with great satisfaction to be able to buy off the rack once again. For far too long, she had been forced to shop at the Big and Tall stores where everything is stretchy and made out of hideous polyester and elastic materials. Sometimes, when frustrated at the limited selection, she had been daring and ordered things online. This would explain the spare room full of brand new clothes that were either too small or a little big but too much of a pain in the behind to return. Clothes really weren't that important, however, since her four hundred pounds of miserable padding had all but confined her to her home in those days.

She snapped herself back to reality and began moving again, past the gleaming jewelry counters filled with cheap imitation chains and baubles and into the children's clothing section. She reached out and touched the frilly little dresses as she passed by and could not resist picking up a pint-sized pair of white, leather tennis shoes, smiling as she placed them back upon the display, remembering she had wanted children once. As a little girl, she had imagined herself all grown up with a handsome, doting husband, four darling children, and a beautiful white French Poodle. She would dream of holidays spent around the dinner table, preparing for a delightful feast as she placed the golden brown turkey in the center of the table. She had pictured herself sitting in front of a crackling fire, holding her husband's hand while the children laughed and squealed beneath a sparkling Christmas tree as they tore the wrapping paper off a huge pile of hand-picked presents. She had dreamt of birthdays, school days, and holidays. Yes, dreams can be wonderful, but life can be cruel.

She steered her cart quickly out of the baby section. Her heart had begun to hurt. In her mind, she suddenly recalled the day Dr. Peterman had told her she was pregnant. She remembered the sheer joy that had enveloped her entire being. She raced home that afternoon to tell her husband and they laughed and then cried. They had celebrated at their favorite restaurant, splurging on steak and lobster, and all was grand in their world. Ahhh, but life is unpredictable. One day you are pregnant and the next day you're not. She had lost the baby. Joy turned to extreme, unbearable sadness and festered into unendurable anger which eventually plunged her into the depths of a deep, dark depression.

Looking back, she could not remember much about those dark days. Life had become a ritual of sleeping and eating, and eating, and eating even more. This caused her to balloon to a colossal three hundred fifty-five pounds with no end in sight. Abandoning her job, her friends, and family, she isolated herself away, shutting out even her husband, who still loved her deeply. For months he was hurt, lost, and lonely and then one day he left with no fanfare. The next two years were spent floundering in self-pity and intense self-loathing.

Lost in thought, she turned a corner a crashed into a dog food display, sending cans of Alpo rolling through the aisles. Embarrassed, she bent down and began gathering the cans just as a startled stock boy rushed to her rescue. Assuring her he would clean up the mess, he sent her along with the hope she would fill up her cart and empty her wallet. Getting back into steering position, she pointed her empty basket toward the back of the store as her mind wandered back to where it had been before the Alpo incident.

A smile lit up her face as she remembered the day her long lost lover had so unexpectedly returned, pounding madly on the front door. When she pulled open the door in tears of extreme and utter happiness, he'd wrapped his arms around her tremendous girth, swearing he'd never leave again if only she'd promise to fight for her life and their love. That day had been the start of an incredibly long journey, three years, in fact; three very long years of struggling through tears, sweat, and counseling for her depression and addiction. Today, she was a brand new woman: happy, healthy, and so very in love.

Glancing up, she saw the pharmacy sign, and her eyes scanned the shelves beneath. Trembling, her hand reached for the inconspicuous little box. She grabbed the package, tossed it into the cart, turned around, and grabbed a second, just to be sure. She did not really need the home pregnancy test. She already knew.

She could feel the tiny soul growing inside of her and she knew this was not just a baby she would give birth to, but a second chance at life, as well. She rolled her cart toward the cashiers at the front of the store, taking a slight detour along the way. Pulling up next to the tiny little tennis shoes, she picked them up and set them gently in the cart and continued walking.

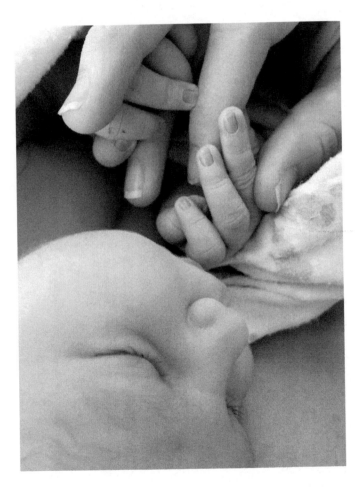

A Restless Winter

"Nope, this was not the life Sydney had hoped for. She longed for the simple existence she had once enjoyed—the quiet refuge of her library, the books, the stories and most of all, the freedom to dream."

Snowflakes drifted from the anemic sky, placing a wet chill in the air that reached inside of Sydney's woolen, winter coat, making her bones ache. Pulling her soft, red scarf tighter around her flushed cheeks, she trudged through the pristine, white snow which had drifted across her driveway during the night. Shivering as she brushed the bothersome slush from her Mercedes, she sighed as she was finally able to slip inside the car and start the engine. As the luxurious sedan purred and came to life, she flipped on the seat warmers and cranked the heat up to full capacity. Sydney then scrambled back out into the January wind to finish the incessant task of brushing and scraping her way through the rest of this year's dreary, disheartening Minnesota winter.

It was part of a wearisome, daily ritual which had somehow, sadly, come to define her colorless, humdrum life. Every day, she rose before the sun, showered, and then downed a cup and a half of very strong, very black coffee. She then proceeded to inch her way down I-394 in a zombie-like state until she drove up the exit to the Richfield Plastic plant. Heading straight for the time clock, Sydney would unenthusiastically punch in while mentally preparing to face another long shift of counting the minutes as they ticked past while doing a job she hated more than anything else in life.

Sydney lived for her afternoon lunch break, when she would hide in a quiet corner of the huge breakroom with a bag of chips and an ice cold Coca Cola. Taking full advantage of this gift of personal time, she would immerse herself into the life of the main character of whatever novel she was engrossed in that week. It was the best hour of the day, and sadly, passed the quickest. She had always loved to read. Books were her passion and she could not even venture to guess how many she had devoured through the years, but she imagined it must have been thousands. Before taking the dreadful job at Richfield, she had spent her days working at the Maple Grove Public Library. For Sydney, it had been a dream job, getting paid to surround herself with shelves upon shelves of glorious books and spending her life just an arm's length away from the magnificent words of the world's finest authors. Walking into the building gave her great joy every morning as the rich scent of the leather-bound classics mingled with the aroma of the fresh newsprint of the *New York Times* and *The Wall Street Journal*. The most amazing part of her job was her privilege to read, at her leisure, any books she chose during down time and slow periods. She had made it her purpose to read a book from a different section of the library every few days and relished in the reality that her choices were perpetual and infinite. The library became her home away from home and she loved just being there. The only problem with her job was the pay had been nominal—awful, in fact—with her earning just a smidge more than minimum wage. Despite her small paycheck, she still considered this to be the best job of all time and can still recall the sense of heartbreak she had felt on her last day working there.

"Richfield Plastic is hiring!" her best friend, Carly, had told her. "It's the first time in nearly ten years!" The news had, in fact, been the talk of the town. Rumor had it that starting pay was eighteen dollars an hour with full benefits and guaranteed overtime, not to mention a substantial raise after a year. Sydney had rushed to the plant to fill out an application along with half of the county and was more than a bit surprised when she received a call to come in for an interview. The man behind the desk studied her application and asked a few questions, but Sydney had nearly fallen out of her chair when he told her to report for work on Monday morning, she was hired! She left the building with her head spinning as she thought about paying off all of her debts. She would be able to afford a townhouse in a better neighborhood and as she walked out to the very back of the parking lot, where she had hidden her rusted out Chevy, Sydney promised herself a new car.

In preparation for her first day of training, Sydney had gone out and bought a new outfit for herself. She was excited to make a good first impression but was very disappointed when her supervisor handed her a Richfield Plastics uniform upon walking in the door. It was the smallest size they carried but since it was made for a man, it hung off her body like the flannel shirt on Uncle Pete's scarecrow. She would have shuddered had she known she would spend most of the next eight years in one of those hideous uniforms.

The days only got worse from there. The job was tedious, the shift was long, and she drove home exhausted most nights. Believing it would get better, Sydney returned day after dreary day, until she found herself, nearly a decade later, still punching into the same old, tired time clock, seeing the same weary faces, and living the same dull and lonely life. Where had all of the years gone? Looking back, she had no real memories, friends, or loved ones. Yes, she drove an expensive car... to work and back. She lived in a swanky new apartment in the very desirable Lakeview Estates, though all she ever seemed to do there was laundry and sleep. Her bank account had grown substantially over time, as had her 401K account after many years of sixty-hour work weeks, raises, and overtime. Sydney's home was full of all of the latest and greatest newfangled gadgets and full of costly furniture, yet with all of this stuff, she still lived an empty, lonesome life. Friends and family had stopped calling long ago since she was never home and when she was, she was too exhausted to entertain or socialize. Nope, this was not the life Sydney had hoped for. She longed for the simple existence she had once enjoyed—the quiet refuge of her library, the books, the stories and most of all, the freedom to dream.

Sydney headed gloomily up the exit while the snow continued to tumble from the sky. Upon reaching the plant, she heaved a heavy sigh as she rolled through the towering steel gates. With a dark mood and a sinking heart, she pulled into a parking space. Staring at the massive, red brick building which loomed ominously before her, she felt her head begin to swim as a surge of nausea filled her throat. Cascades of snow began to envelope the car. The flakes melted quickly on the warm windshield, running swiftly down the glass, and still she remained, sedentary and sullen. Reaching for the ignition, she frowned and then let her hand drop into her lap as she sank back into the rich leather seat of the idling Mercedes. With her mind racing, she sat in silence and contemplated her future. In her mind's eye, she envisioned living the same lonely life, working the same monotonous job, day after dismal day, where she would eventually wither up and grow old before her time.

At that precise moment, something transpired—a thought, a wish, a notion; she could not be sure. Considering her future, Sydney suddenly understood the existence she was immersed in was not living, it was dying. This plant, this place—this *job*—stole one precious day from her limited allotment every single time she passed through these gates. Today, the nightmare would end and her intended life would begin. Realizing she had paid her dues and sacrificed priceless years of her life, she cultivated a plan. Somewhere out there, in a charming, coastal town, there was a quaint little bookstore for sale. Sydney would collect her hard-earned money, pack up her things, and go and find it. Once located, she would set up shop, getting to know the folks and history of her new community. There would be a delightful little house near the water with a white picket fence, a porch swing, and a flower garden. In this place she would grow much more than roses and tulips; she would let her spirit flourish, as well.

Sydney still stared at the factory before her, but for the first time in a very long time, she smiled. As she reached out and shifted the car into reverse, she was overcome with an intense feeling of both relief and excitement. As she maneuvered her car back through those imprisoning gates, she resisted the urge to call her supervisor, thinking to herself, *No call, no show, no turning back.*

Unbreakable

"They will smile as they take, acquire, and procure much more than you ever intended to bestow upon them. Enough is never enough."

Watch out for them. They are cunning and crafty, shrewd and deceitful, and so very skilled at concealing their motives. Without warning, they will latch on to your character and begin stealing your soul. They will convince and remind you, every single day, just how lucky you are to have them in your life, when in all reality, *they* are indeed the lucky one to have found such a generous, caring soul to befriend them. They will smile as they take, acquire, and procure much more than you ever intended to bestow upon them. Enough is never enough. Even when they have pilfered your last shred of dignity, they rummage for more. Becoming quite skilled at unearthing the sad, disheartened, and lonely, they push past their insecurities and feed upon the misery of their prey. They will vigorously *protect* you from all that is adverse or offending, but only because they want all that you have, for themselves, much like a vulture picking at your bones. Slowly but surely, they will steal every bit of confidence, self-respect, and dignity you have managed to hang on to after a lifetime of struggle and despair. Believing them to be loyal, truthful, and kind, you entrust them with your secrets, your insecurities, and your heart, hoping and believing they will be there for you when hit your rock bottom. Of course, they are not. You sit there alone, struggling in anguish to climb your way out, never even realizing they have moved on to find a new feeding ground.

The pattern is the same and you sit in silence, shaking your head, watching the destruction from a front row seat, wanting to help, yet knowing the newest prey is hypnotized and mesmerized just as you were. When it is all said and done, you will reach out to comfort the poor soul and you will bond together in shared and similar misery, taking strength from one another as you attempt to rebuild your lives. It will be a difficult journey, but take solace in the reliable realization that Karma is a hungry beast—a fearless predator with steadfast patience and fortitude. Karma is fierce in that it always, always wins. Remember, too, that time will repair your crushed spirit as it restores your innocent love for life, and don't ever forget that you, my friend, are unbreakable.

About Alana Marie

In 1994 I made a huge career change. I quit my job and decided to open a bar. Not just any bar, but a gay/lesbian show bar. I immersed my entire being in the nightclub scene and yes indeed, it was a "gay" old time I had. I found myself living a life of excess. I drank too much, ate too much, partied too much, dated too many women to count and spent much more money than I had. After 17 years of abuse, my body almost self-destructed. At one point, I found myself weighing in at 528 pounds, an alcoholic, broke and alone. I remember the night when a friend drove me home after pounding down a fifth of liquor at my club. It was a freezing cold January night. I stepped out of the car and slipped and fell in the driveway. I shattered my wrist in three places that night. Unable to lift my 400 pound bulk up off the ground, even with the help of my friend, I sat there in the freezing snow until after about an hour, I eventually crawled into my house and fell asleep on the floor. I woke up the next morning and sat there on my little corner of "rock bottom" feeling very sorry for myself. I was repulsed and ashamed of what I had become. On January 15, 2012, I had an epiphany. I was forced to face the reality of my mortality and I was mortified.

RESOURCES

Check out Alana's website

www.pickastrugglecupcake.com

Social Media:

Follow Alana on Facebook and Twitter

https://www.facebook.com/authoralanamariefaulk

https://twitter.com/AlanaMarieFaulk

Join the Pick A Struggle Book Club Page

https://www.facebook.com/groups/pickastrugglebookclub

Join the Pick A Struggle Community – a personal development and support group

http://www.pickastruggleenterprises.com

Speaker: Looking for a dynamic speaker? Alana is available for keynote presentations, breakout sessions, workshops and customer programs. Contact her at Alana@pickastruggle.com

Alana Marie

25311981R00125